Additional Praise for *Business Secrets of the Trappist Monks*

"This book is both quietly provocative and groundbreaking. With great simplicity, August Turak unlocks monastic 'secrets' that go to the core of succeeding in an economic era in which authenticity and passion have become key. Who knew the monks had so many things right?"

—*Tom Freston*, former CEO of Viacom and MTV Networks

"*Business Secrets of the Trappist Monks* is sure to be a business classic. It is a compelling and important tutorial on how to build authentically sustainable companies. Turak's stories and examples are magical, yet the philosophical ideas they're founded on resonate with truth. It is a must-read for the thoughtful executive."

—*Mark Booth*, former chairman and
CEO of NetJets Europe

"This is an eloquent, powerful book that accentuates the power of trust and the surprising gift that selfless leadership can bring to institutions. Turak expertly shows how Trappist ways and wisdom connect character to the art of leadership, and how this unique approach can be helpful in our current thinking about leadership, business, and the meaning of our own lives. New insights and ancient truth blend in this remarkable book by a remarkable teacher."

—*Will Willimon*, Duke Divinity School and
author of *Sinning Like a Christian:
A New Look at the Seven Deadly Sins*

"This inspirational book presents a different view of business leadership and success that is important for serious and aspiring business leaders to take into consideration. Turak also has a narrative voice that is both genuine and authoritative, and he has thoughtfully organized 'take-aways' throughout the book into lists that will be extremely useful for readers."

—*Lindsay Thompson*, John Hopkins Carey Business School

BUSINESS SECRETS
of the
TRAPPIST MONKS

One CEO's
Quest for Meaning
and Authenticity

August Turak

4 **Columbia Business School**
Publishing

Columbia University Press
Publishers Since 1893
New York   Chichester, West Sussex
cup.columbia.edu
Copyright © 2013 August Turak
Paperback edition, 2015
All rights reserved

Library of Congress Cataloging-in-Publication Data

Turak, August.
  The business secrets of the Trappist monks : one CEO's quest for meaning
and authenticity / August Turak.
      pages   cm
  ISBN 978-0-231-16062-9 (cloth : alk. paper)—ISBN 978-0-231-16063-6 (pbk. :
alk. paper)—ISBN 978-0-231-53522-9 (e-book)
  1. Business ethics—United States.   2. Success in business—United States.
3. Abbey of Our Lady of Mepkin (Moncks Corner, S.C.)   I. Title.
  HF5387.5.U6T87   2013
  174'.4—dc23

2012050815

∞
Columbia University Press books are printed on permanent and durable acid-free paper.
This book is printed on paper with recycled content.
Printed in the United States of America

c 10 9 8 7 6 5 4 3
p 10 9 8 7 6 5 4 3

COVER IMAGE:
Photo by William C. Carter, III
www.flickr.com/photos/billcarter

COVER DESIGN:
Milenda Nan Ok Lee

References to websites (URLs) were accurate at the time of writing. Neither the author
nor Columbia University Press is responsible for URLs that may have expired or changed
since the manuscript was prepared.

For

Dom Francis Kline

and

all my brothers

of

Our Lady of Mepkin Abbey

-heroes journey related to
Greet works

CONTENTS

Preface

ix

1

The Economic Miracle of Mepkin Abbey

1

2

What We All Really Want

15

3

The End of Selfishness

33

4

Goat Rodeos and the Transformational Organization

45

5

Mission

57

6

Selflessness and Community

77

Contents

7

Excellence for the Sake of Excellence

91

8

Ethical Standards, or,

Why Good Things Happen for Good People

115

9

Faith

127

10

The Power of Trust

139

11

Self-knowledge and Authenticity

153

12

Living the Life

169

PREFACE

FOR 1,500 YEARS monasteries all over the world have been calling men and women to a life of prayer and work according to the Rule of St. Benedict. The monastic motto *ora et labora* ("pray and work") tells us that these twin pillars of the monastic life are of equal importance—so much so, in fact, that for a Trappist monk, work is a form of prayer and prayer is a form of work. But while many authors, like Thomas Merton, have taken us behind the cloister walls to explore monastic prayer, very little has been written about the "work" half of the monastic equation. Similarly, although much has been written about the tremendous intellectual debt that Western civilization owes monasticism for preserving Greek philosophy and drama during the Dark Ages, very few have explored the highly successful business methodologies that the monks have preserved and prospered by for centuries.

This book takes a step toward redressing this imbalance by bringing these neglected monastic business secrets to light and sharing them with a wider world. This is not a disinterested academic treatise on monastic business practices; rather, it is a highly personal, nuts-and-bolts account of the business lessons I have learned over seventeen years while living and working with the monks of Mepkin Abbey in Moncks Corner, South Carolina, as a frequent monastic guest. Further, by incorporating case studies drawn from my own career and from the example of other successful companies and organizations, I hope to show you how to apply these monastic lessons to a secular marketplace in order to run a more profitable business and have a more successful career. Perhaps what is more important, I believe that if you take these lessons to heart, you will also enjoy a more meaningful and satisfying personal life. I feel fairly safe in making these assertions because I know that these Trappist secrets don't work just for monks; they worked for me as well.

Most of my monastic research was conducted firsthand while getting my hands dirty working alongside the monks, but I'm not alone in my fascination with the business success of the Trappists. An article in *USA Today* about the beer-brewing Belgian monks of St. Sixtus Abbey provides a wonderful three-sentence summary of Trappist business success, saying: "Piety, not profit, is what these monks seek. The St. Sixtus monks break every rule in Business 101 except attention to quality. And therein may lie the secret to their success."

At first glance this analysis may seem woefully incomplete. Of course delivering a quality product is crucial to the success of a business, but what about pricing, positioning, accounting, human resources, cash management, distribution, marketing, procurement, competition, R&D, customer support, government regulations, patent protection, and access to capital? All these things (and many more) are also necessary—not only for producing a quality product in the first place but for making sure that this product can consistently find a market. However, a closer consideration of the phrase "attention to quality" should help us overcome these qualms. Quality doesn't just apply to the relative merits of what are commonly referred to as "products." Attention to quality also implies a qualitative rather than a quantitative approach to business, and it is only through this much larger lens that we can begin to see how the monks regularly break the rules of Business 101 and do it so successfully.

For more than a hundred years, the dominant trends in business have been quantitative and analytic. In 1911 Frederick Taylor published his seminal *Principles of Scientific Management,* and ever since then economists, consultants, pundits, and legions of business-school professors have been trying to wrest business from the clutches of art in the hope of turning it into a science. Unfortunately, the significant dividends that this quantitative approach has produced have often come at the expense of the more qualitative aspects of business—things like mission, purpose, values, principles, integrity, ethics, service, and people, which, the monks would argue, are even more critical to success. These qualitative aspects of business are what the monks have mastered, and the author of the *USA Today* article aptly sums up all this monastic know-how with a single word: *piety.*

Piety comes from the Latin word for "duty," and according to Webster's dictionary, piety in its broadest sense encompasses the duty we owe to parents, country, and our fellow man, and to any noble undertaking that transcends our purely selfish motivations. For Trappist monks, seeking "piety, not profit" means faithfully paying attention to the sacred duty they owe not only to God but to their customers, lay employees, vendors, local community, each other, the environment, and mankind in general. It is the dutiful, or "prayerful," way in which the monks attend to these qualitative aspects of business that is the overarching secret to their success. And the paradoxical theme that runs throughout this book is that the monks are successful not *despite* the fact that they seek piety, not profits, but *because* they do.

Nothing in this book denigrates the quantitative approach to business or treats it as something superfluous. As a business executive and entrepreneur, I've spent countless hours poring over spreadsheets, flowcharts, research, and "the numbers" generally, and I know some monks who are second to none in this regard. Yet if one of the purposes of this book is to redress the imbalance between prayer and work in the world's appraisal of monasticism, another is to redress the gross imbalance between the quantitative and qualitative approaches to business.

I use the phrase *service and selflessness* to describe the monastic business model throughout this book, and the key to successfully applying this Trappist model to our secular business challenges is authenticity. *Authenticity* is the latest business buzzword: we hear of authentic businesses, authentic leadership, authentic products, and authentic brands. But while often positioned as the "next big thing" in business, authenticity is nothing new to the monks: Trappist monks have been building authentic businesses, leaders, brands, and products for more than a thousand years. Trappist authenticity shows up in three distinct areas of the monastic way of life and business, and throughout this book, we will be returning again and again to these crucial areas. The first is mission, the second is personal transformation, and the third is community.

Mission

A QUALITATIVE APPROACH TO business means articulating a high, overarching mission worthy of being piously served. To be authentic, this mission must genuinely drive the decision making that in turn determines even the tiniest activities of the enterprise. Trappist monks don't *have* a mission, something to be kept safely tucked in a drawer until the annual meeting rolls around or someone innocently asks about it. Instead the monks *live* their mission every single day. It is this critical distinction that is so often missing in our secular organizations—and in our personal lives as well.

Personal Transformation

AUTHENTICITY IS NOT a technique that can be mastered and then manipulated for our own ends. It is not something we can turn on and off at a moment's notice as the situation requires. Authentic businesses, leaders, brands, and products can only be created by authentic people, and that is exactly why the monks are so good at it. In the *USA Today* article, the St. Sixtus brewmaster, Brother Joris, is quoted as saying, "You do not become a saint just by entering a monastery." *Saintliness* is just a religious term for authenticity, and the monastic way of life is designed to take ordinary people and transform them into authentic individuals. One of the secrets to the monks' success is that they value personal authenticity above everything else. The authentic brands, products, and leaders that the Trappists produce are merely the by-products of this continual movement toward authenticity. If we want the business benefits that only authenticity can bestow, we must first become authentic individuals. Just how to make this happen in a secular world and in a secular way is a large part of what this book offers.

Community

TRAPPIST BUSINESS SUCCESS RELIES on the cooperative lubrication that only an authentic community can provide. The Trappist mission and individual drive toward authenticity would amount to little were it not for the monks' unwavering commitment to community. It is the constant mutual reinforcement and beneficial peer pressure of community that keeps the monastic mission front and center and does most of the heavy lifting involved in personal transformation.

But the communal commitment that drives the Trappist way of life is not circumscribed by the cloister walls that enclose the monastery. The Trappists' communal embrace encompasses customers, retreatants, government regulators, their neighbors in the local community, and—through ceaseless prayer—all of us. All these constituencies are authentically treated as "brothers and sisters," and this is a critical component of Trappist business success.

The Trappist commitment to mission, individual transformation, and community are all intertwined; these three elements feed back on each other in a virtuous cycle that produces what we often describe in business as "culture." Once again, it is the critical distinction between an authentic culture and an inauthentic culture that makes all the difference to success. Creating and maintaining an authentic business culture is fraught with difficulty, but how to do it is perhaps the most important thing you will learn from the monks you meet in this book.

The Greek philosopher Archimedes famously said, "Give me a long enough lever and a place to stand, and I will move the world." The same might be said of the business, professional, and personal "leverage" the Trappists have to offer us all if we take their secrets to heart.

THE PROBLEM WITH LIFE is that it must be lived forward and only understood backward. When I first drove through the gates of Mepkin Abbey back in 1996, the last thing on my mind was writing a book on Trappist business acumen. I was the CEO of a software start-up undergoing the most severe personal crisis of my life, and I was turning to the monks for the psychological and spiritual help that I so sorely needed and which they so graciously provided. I owe so much more than just this book to the monks of Mepkin Abbey.

It was only eight years later and entirely by accident that I began writing about the monks of Mepkin. In 1987 I started an organization called the Self Knowledge Symposium (SKS) to help college students at local universities answer the perennial question, What is the life worth living? In 2004 a former student got in touch to suggest that I write an essay for the John Templeton Foundation's Power of Purpose essay contest, but when I clicked on the link embedded in his e-mail, I was dismayed. In 3,500 words or less, I had to answer the question, What is the purpose of life? I'd never written anything for publication before, and the contest was open to professional writers and previously published material. Worse, the deadline for submissions for the yearlong contest was barely a week away.

I took a crack at it anyway, but after several days of head scratching, I had nothing to show for my efforts but a mountain of crumpled paper and false starts. I was venting my frustration over the phone with another former student when he suggested, "Hell, Augie, why don't you just write up that story about Brother John and Mepkin Abbey that you love telling so much?"

After a couple days of frantic writing, I submitted my essay a few hours before the deadline and then forgot about it, only to get a phone call six months later: my essay, "Brother John," had won the grand prize and $100,000 besides. I was so shell-shocked that it took the caller a full five minutes to convince me I had actually won.

Several years later and almost on a whim, I decided to write what amounted to a white paper on the business lessons I'd learned from the monks over the years. Although not intended for publication, it found its way to Fred Allen, the leadership editor for Forbes.com, and he asked for permission to publish it as a four-part article. The article, "Business Secrets of the Trappists," was very successful, and it was Fred Allen who urged me to turn the article into a book. And it was another happy accident—a chance meeting between a friend and my wonderful publisher, Myles Thompson—that led me to Columbia University Press and all the amazing people there who made this book possible.

It was a long series of largely serendipitous events that turned me into a writer, and herein lies another important secret that the monks have to teach. In the manner of the monks of St. Sixtus, I have broken every rule of How to Become a Writer 101, and throughout this book I argue that authentic success—whether personal, professional, or organizational—is usually only the by-product, the trailing indicator, of serving a mission that is bigger than yourself. The Trappist lesson here is that you cannot "game the system" that the monks have to offer. If your goal in reading this book is to find a shortcut to success by merely imitating the monks and their business strategies, you will find little of value. Above all else the secret to duplicating Trappist success lies in sincerity—or at least a sincere desire to become a more sincere person in every aspect of your life.

I have worked very hard throughout this book to apply Trappist principles in a nondogmatic, nonsectarian, and nonreligious way. I sincerely believe that these Trappist secrets will work for you whether you are a believer or not—as long as your heart is in "the right place." I would be less than candid, however, if I did not reveal that I believe there is something to the Trappist business model that transcends any "formula," no matter how well that formula may be articulated. We golfers like to say that the secret to a great round is "just let the hole get in the way of the ball," and this is just a golfer's version of the religious admonition to "let go and let God." Trappist monks don't just make success happen; they also let success happen, and this may be the deepest and most profound secret they have to share. You can call it grace if you are so inclined, or luck if you're not, but there is something almost magical about the Trappist Way that seems to attract success whether you are a monk or not. Looking back over all the happy accidents that led to this book and so much of my own business success, I can clearly see this Trappist grace (or luck) at work. As a result I must confess that I have become a "true believer," and that perhaps my most important goal in writing this book is my hope that you may learn how to invite this Trappist magic into your own life and business ventures as well.

BUSINESS SECRETS
of the
TRAPPIST MONKS

THE ECONOMIC MIRACLE
OF MEPKIN ABBEY

LOCATED JUST OUTSIDE Charleston, South Carolina, the 3,132 oak-studded acres that make up Our Lady of Mepkin Abbey roll gently toward the Atlantic Ocean. Early each morning except Sunday, right after the fourth daily monastic service, Terce, I'd borrow a bicycle from the monastery's pool and, surrounded by four or five Trappist monks and their wind-whipped habits, I'd pedal off for Mepkin Abbey's "eggery," or grading house. With the rising sun shimmering off the Cooper River, my mile-long bike ride through fragrant gardens, moss-strewn live oaks, and cool salt air would just about lift the last vestige of drowsiness left over from rising for Vigils at three o'clock in the morning. At the grading house, I would join Father Malachy at the end of the line just in time to watch Brother Nick flip the switch that brought the clattering conveyor to life. Soon the recently harvested eggs from 40,000 of Brother Joseph's pampered poultry would be snaking their way around the cavernous concrete-block building. At stations along the slowly moving conveyor, the eggs were cleaned, checked for imperfections, graded from small to jumbo, put into cartons, and packed into large cardboard crates on their way to the shelves of local grocery stores. I liked to think they were whisked on their way with a "blessing in every box," but when I suggested embossing each carton with this motto to Mepkin's business manager, Father Stan, he only smiled and gently rolled his eyes.

And as I worked, I often found myself absently wondering how Father Malachy supernaturally managed to beat me to work every day.

Father Malachy was a bearded, slight, and slightly stooped monk well into his eighties. His blue eyes were gentle, and the thick blue veins lacing his delicate hands were perfectly suited to hands that had spent the better part of a lifetime clasped in prayer. My job was packing the cartons of eggs into boxes as they spat off the line, and day after day Father Malachy unfolded, shaped, and stacked the large cardboard crates that I busily stuffed and shoved into the cooler. Despite his diligence, patience, and prayer-worn hands, as we became friendly, I saw only a simple man and simple monk engaged in a simple task.

One day I jokingly mentioned that he always had two helpings of ice cream whenever it was served in the refectory. "I used to eat three," he whispered conspiratorially. "But the abbot took me aside and said, 'Father Malachy, do you think a man your age should be eating so much ice cream?' Now I only eat two."

Then, on another day, Malachy mentioned that several years earlier, someone had donated to the abbey a big box of theological tomes written in French. Calling Malachy to his office, the abbot asked him to write English summaries of these books for the library.

"Well," Father Malachy said softly, "Francis thought I spoke French, but I didn't. But he's so busy, I didn't bring it up. I just stayed up late for a few months, taught myself French, read the books, and wrote the summaries." Then he humbly returned to his boxes, leaving me slack jawed with envy and abject awe.

Little by little I found out many not-so-simple things about this simple man. I learned that when Our Lady of Mepkin found herself short of priests, Malachy mastered all the intellectual requirements for the priesthood on his own, and in short order, without ever leaving the monastery. I discovered that Father Malachy was a favorite confessor for the other monks because of his keen insights into the human heart. And when neither the abbot nor Mepkin's amazing cantor and Irish tenor, Father Aelred, were present at one of the monastery's eight daily services, it was the musically self-taught Father Malachy with his pitch pipe who led the community in hymns and the chanting of the psalms. As more and more such revelations seeped out over the years, my awe and affection for this humble man grew apace.

Then one day a phone call relayed the news that Father Malachy was dead. Racing to the monastery, I arrived barely in time for the funeral. During his eulogy Abbot Francis told us that only ten days previously, Father Malachy, complaining of pain, had been taken to the hospital for tests. He was riddled with cancer, and it fell to Francis to convey the news that there was no hope and very little time left. But when Francis told Father Malachy he was dying, Father Malachy didn't even blink. He just leaned over from his hospital bed, stroked Dom Francis on the arm, and, with a gentle smile, softly said, "Oh, that's all right." Unable to continue his eulogy, Francis broke down at the altar.

As Mass ended Father Stan whispered that the brothers wanted me to carry the crucifix in Father Malachy's funeral procession to the cemetery. The coffin remained open, and when we arrived, a white handkerchief was pinned to his habit to cover Father Malachy's face. Then his body was lifted by straps from the coffin and slowly lowered into his coffinless grave. Prayers were said, and one by one each of us sprinkled a handful of monastic soil into the grave.

As the monastic community slowly dispersed, I found myself walking with Brother Robert. When it was time to go our separate ways, I told him how much I loved Father Malachy and admired the heroic way he had faced his own death—comforting someone else instead of seeking comfort for himself. Brother Robert merely smiled, gave me a hug, and turned away. But after a few steps, the black cowl on his hooded head slowly turned. "You know," he said, "Everyone wants to die like a Trappist. No one wants to live like one."

MEPKIN ABBEY, once the estate of Henry and Clare Boothe Luce, is now a sanctuary for 25 or so Trappist monks living a life of contemplative prayer according to the arduous Rule of St. Benedict. The first time I drove through the gates, in 1996, the monastery's beauty, tranquility, and poignant silence instantly settled over me like a magical mist. It was as if Mepkin's invisible gatekeeper had insisted on taking the weight of the world from my shoulders in lieu of a toll.

I have been returning to Mepkin ever since, sometimes for months at a time. As a monastic guest, I wear a gray habit and temporarily live the life of a Trappist monk. But while I go primarily for spiritual reasons, as a businessman and entrepreneur, I am fascinated by a worldly aspect of the monastic life. Mepkin and other monasteries throughout the world run highly successful businesses, and over the years I have found myself coming back again and again to some basic questions about them.

How do a couple of dozen aged monks at Mepkin, working only part time and largely in silence, achieve such amazing business success? How does Mepkin Abbey inspire ordinary people such as Father Malachy to achieve such extraordinary results? Why have monastic businesses thrived for more than 1,500 years when modern corporate success is so fleeting? How do monasteries produce and sell "me, too" commodities like fruitcakes, beer, eggs, mushrooms, and cheese with the kind of pricing power usually associated with dominant brands? Why does demand for these prosaic products consistently outstrip supply? How do monks compete so successfully in the open market while maintaining only the highest ethical standards and commitment to quality? And, most importantly, how can we apply these Trappist techniques to our secular corporations, nonprofits, families, and even our personal lives with equally explosive results?

The short answer is that the monks have discovered an amazing secret: it is in our own self-interest to forget our self-interest. Paradoxically, the reason for Mepkin's business success is that the monks are not actually in business at all. Instead they are utterly committed to a high, overarching mission and a management philosophy this book will refer to as *service and selflessness*. Business success for the monks is merely the by-product of a life well lived.

The Rule of St. Benedict urges monasteries to be self-sufficient and self-supporting communities, and Trappists accomplish this primarily through manual labor. Indeed, the Rule of St. Benedict calls monks to manual labor as an essential aspect of the monastic experience. *Orare est laborare*—to pray is to work—is a principle new monks learn quickly at Mepkin Abbey. Once the home of 40,000 egg-laying chickens, Mepkin recently transitioned into raising mushrooms. The monks sell organic fertilizer, run a gift shop, and manage a huge tract of renewable timber as well.

The land, an antebellum rice plantation once owned by Henry Laurens, the fifth president of the Continental Congress, was a gift from the Luce family back in the 1940s. It came with a magnificent garden along the Cooper River, which the monks meticulously maintain. Henry and Clare Boothe Luce are buried there. The abbey has a beautiful church, a wonderful library, a conference center, a guest center, and more than a dozen immaculate retreat houses.

The brothers entertain a constant stream of retreatants, guests, and sightseers while cooking for themselves and caring for their aged and infirm in a spotless, state-of-the-art infirmary. The Trappist vow of stability that, Father Francis said, turns monks into "lovers of the place" is expressed in a passionate interest in the environment. As a result the monks are painstakingly restoring the land and a long-lost cemetery for the plantation's slaves to their pristine state.

Impressive as all this sounds, what is most amazing is that all these accomplishments represent the part-time effort of a couple of dozen elderly men living and working together, mostly in silence. The monks rise at three in the morning and attend eight communal services a day. They spend hours in solitary prayer, contemplation, and sacred reading. Because their mission includes this commitment to a life of contemplative prayer, the monks typically work only four hours a day.

Yet if we are impressed by the monks because they manage to accomplish so much *despite* their single-minded dedication to their mission, we are making a common but cardinal error. It is *because* of their focus on mission and selfless service that they operate a multimillion-dollar enterprise with a degree of frictionless efficiency that would drive most profit-driven executives to distraction with envy. And this book will show that if we are willing to learn from the monks, we can do the same.

According to the *Wall Street Journal,* the monks of St. Sixtus Abbey in Belgium make a beer that is "among the most highly prized in the world." Without the benefit of advertising or even labels on their bottles, the monks sell 60,000 cases a year. Cars line up for miles outside the gates, stuffed with beer lovers hoping to take home their two-case limit of a very limited supply. Yet despite *USA Today*'s contention that the "St. Sixtus monks break every rule in Business 101 except attention to quality," the *Wall Street Journal* argued that the biggest business problem the monks of St. Sixtus face is the "spiritual hangover" brought on by the market's "insatiable" demand for their product. And it is not only St. Sixtus that is thriving—the Trappist beer made by the brothers of Scourmont, also in Belgium, brings in $50 million a year. Closer to home, *Time* magazine reported that the Trappist monks of St. Joseph's Abbey in Spencer, Massachusetts, sell 1,230,000 jars of their Trappist Preserves every year through grocery stores all over the country.

But while these figures emphatically make the case for Trappist business acumen, the real secret to monastic success is neatly captured by what Brother Joris, the brewmaster for St. Sixtus, told the *Wall Street Journal*: "We sell beer to live, and not vice versa." The monks are not profit-driven people who happen to think about higher purpose once in a while. They are people passionately committed to their mission of selfless service to God and others who happen to have a business. Business success for the monks is merely the by-product of living a life of service and selflessness. This radical reorientation of priorities, a Trappist secret we will refer to again and again as *aiming past the target*, makes all the difference.

Service and selflessness lies at the heart of the monastic tradition and every Trappist business success. This 1,500-year-old monastic tradition represents an ancient yet emergent socioeconomic model that can teach us how to keep what is positive and productive about capitalism while transcending its ethical limitations and internal contradictions.

This book draws on my seventeen years of experience with the monks of Mepkin, my background as a corporate executive and entrepreneur, the rare privilege I enjoyed as the protégé of one of the founders of the IBM Executive School, and the example of a host of other transformational organizations to demonstrate that service and selflessness not only produces dramatically more successful organizations but happier employees and customers as well.

When people like Ayn Rand argue that we are all selfish and that the "invisible hand" of capitalism emerges from this selfishness, they are not completely wrong, but only half right. Every child endlessly shouting "Mine!" starts out selfish and moves toward selflessness as he matures. The trajectory of the human race—what we call *civilization*—is a similar movement from the selfishness of kings toward the selflessness of democracy, and history's economic models share this halting trajectory from win/lose toward win/win. Capitalism is not as selfish as the mercantilist system that preceded it, and mercantilism in turn was a big step forward from feudalism.

The current worldwide economic crisis is often blamed on the greed, selfishness, and unethical excesses of unbridled free-market capitalism. To a large extent, I agree with this analysis, even though as a businessman and entrepreneur, I love our free-market system. Most of us assume, however, that greed, selfishness, and unethical behavior are intrinsic to free markets, capitalism, and "profit." And since capitalism has proved to be the most productive economic model the world has yet seen, this has led many to conclude that all we can do is manage a painful deal with the devil. Capitalism takes on the role of a wild and dangerous animal sharing our house; an animal we can live neither with nor without. This analysis assumes that this selfish beast can never be tamed, so it must be constantly restrained lest it suddenly turn on its master with the kind of disastrous consequences we have recently experienced.

Unfortunately, this description of capitalism traps us in a painful dichotomy; things like higher purpose, putting people first, and looking out for the customer are invariably at odds with "profit" and "bottom line" considerations. In this war the bottom line always seems to win, and higher goals are perpetually damned to the realm of altruism. There these higher goals languish, their only advocates the bully pulpit of corporate guilt and futile appeals to mankind's "better nature."

As I spent more and more time living and working alongside the monks of Mepkin Abbey, I began to realize that at heart they are living an ancient yet emergent economic model that rejects the assumption that capitalism and selfless service are essentially at odds with one another and mutually exclusive. The monks of Mepkin and agnostics like Warren Buffett alike have been wildly successful in business not despite their fanatical commitment to the highest principles but because of them. The counterintuitive secret that the monks, Buffett, and the world's greatest salespeople have discovered is that the more successfully we forget our selfish motivations, the more successful we become.

If this analysis is correct, then our task, though still daunting, is no longer just endless, acrimonious, time-consuming, and expensive trade-offs between capitalism and socialism, competition and cooperation, profit and nonprofit, growing people and using people, free markets and government regulation, altruistic motivations and selfish motivations. Instead we must transcend these false dichotomies by conclusively demonstrating that service and selflessness is not all "motherhood and fluff." We must prove that selfless service can be more than a thinly veiled PR campaign and corporate-recruitment strategy masking as "give back." For, as Warren Buffett, the monks, and my personal experience as a salesman, executive, and entrepreneur will show, service and selflessness will lead to businesses that are more profitable and productive than those we have today. Service and selflessness is not about sacrificing growth and profitability for some abstract and elusive "common good." It is just damn good business.

This model does not envision dismantling the capitalist system and the "profit" that has lifted so many out of poverty. Service and selflessness transcends all the painful trade-offs listed above. It does so by tapping into the universal longing we all have for a mission that is so much bigger than ourselves that it transforms us, both individually and collectively, from selfish to selfless people.

EARLY ONE MORNING a monk I'd never seen before arrived at the egg grading house and took his place beside me on the line. Several hours later the monastery's antediluvian conveyor system suddenly died, and work ground to a halt. While Brother John—with the patience of Job, the faith of Abraham, and the biggest hammer I've ever seen—was trying to work yet another miracle, I discovered that my line mate was from a monastery in New Zealand, just passing through on his way to a conference.

I casually remarked that I had recently read an article about New Zealand's free-market reforms and the economic benefits they were producing. Unexpectedly my comment provoked a jeremiad on the dislocation and unemployment these "so-called reforms" were producing in his country.

Miffed by what I felt was a note of personal antipathy behind his speech, I countered that my own company was having trouble finding people willing to work. We had recently hired five students for the summer to do market research at double the minimum wage, and within days they had all quit.

"Maybe they don't like making phone calls all day long," he interrupted.

"Maybe I don't like packing eggs," I retorted in the same tone of voice.

His features softened. "What, you don't enjoy working here?"

"I never think about it," I whispered, startled into the truth by the change in his tone and demeanor. "I just do what Brother John asks me to do, and I'm just so grateful he lets me do it."

"Of course," he said through a widening smile, "nothing else really matters, does it? It's the Trappist way, brother, the Trappist way."

The next thing I knew, we were hugging, and just as suddenly the inanimate machinery around us yielded to Brother John's supernatural hammering. The resurrected conveyor staggered forward under its own power, and I staggered back to work conveyed by something much bigger than myself.

This is the power of service and selflessness, or what my brother from New Zealand called the Trappist way. In a few moments, all the barriers of politics, economics, nationality, and personal experience keeping us apart were put in their proper perspective by our mutual commitment to the monastic mission. Our incompatibilities of opinion and outlook did not go away, nor were they reconciled—after all, creativity depends on individuality, diversity of opinion, and honest disagreement. Instead our differences were transcended by a mission that was bigger than our selfish concerns.

Similarly, if we want to transcend capitalism rather than dismantle it, we must amend the flawed philosophy of people like Ayn Rand. They assume that human beings, and therefore capitalism, are static models driven solely by self-interest. What I'll argue throughout this book is that mankind is actually a dynamic "model" longing to selflessly "surrender" to serving something bigger than ourselves. And when, like the monks, we combine this urge toward selflessness with free enterprise, we discover an economic model that overcomes many of the limitations of capitalism.

For example, all great salespeople know that the more they make it their mission to "forget" themselves, their product, and their commissions and concentrate on serving their customers' needs, the more sales they make. The commissions take care of themselves. When entire corporations relentlessly focus on selflessly serving customers, profits take care of themselves as well. The best leaders realize that the more they focus on making other people successful, the more successful they become.

Many people think of a monastery as a static model as well: a place where supernaturally gifted "holy men" go to passively live out their days in blissful tranquility. Still others take the more cynical view that the monastery is a static model full of selfish men hiding from their worldly responsibilities.

Instead, the secret to Our Lady of Mepkin's business success is that she offers a dynamic model: an incubator for ordinary men longing to be permanently transformed from selfish to selfless people by the monastic mission and methodology. And the challenges inherent in achieving this transformation are anything but trivial.

Sunday is a day of rest at Mepkin, and on Sunday afternoons the grounds are dotted with monks in black-hooded habits over long, white albs taking long, leisurely walks, usually accompanied by one of their brothers. I was taking such a stroll one Sunday with a novice, an accomplished artist and former teacher of about fifty, still hip deep in the monastic process of formation by which a new recruit is gradually transformed into a monk. We'd been meandering aimlessly and in silence for some time when suddenly he whirled around: "At least you have some idea what goes on here," he said, his eyes blazing. "Most people think it's all peace and tranquility, but it is really so incredibly intense. Every time I think I'm making progress, I catch myself elbowing some ninety-year-old monk out of the way so I can get that last dish of ice cream. This place is just one big mirror; all I have to do is look at these guys to realize just how selfish I still am."

It is the hunger for this transformation from selfishness to self-lessness, for what the monks call *self-transcendence*, that sent this novice—a regular guy, just like me and you—to the monastery in the first place. It is this longing that also produces the kind of passionate commitment to the monastery's business mission that I saw in him every day at work. And when this transformation from selfishness to selflessness finally takes place, we find its full flower in the almost supernatural feats of men like Father Malachy.

This transformation goes by as many names as there are cultures and can be religious, secular, or even both, but the key is that it always produces a more selfless individual. And when the opportunity for this transformation is offered collectively through mission and methodology, it leads to a more successful family, club, nonprofit, or corporation.

Of course the challenges involved in using the monastic model to transform our corporate culture are substantial. The task may seem more daunting and naive than the alternative: fighting an endless rearguard action against selfish corporate greed through draconian regulation, enforcement, and plaintive appeals to mankind's better angels. But whenever I begin losing heart, I try to remember that creating a corporate culture based on selfless service is probably no more unrealistic than the task Adam Smith faced in transforming the even more selfish mercantilistic economic model of his own time. The challenges the first pioneers faced in transforming barter economies into money economies must have been more daunting still. And our task pales almost to insignificance when compared with that of the first practitioner of the dismal science of economics, lost in the mists of time, who took his life in his hands by suggesting to his fellow warriors that it might be more profitable in the long run to trade with the neighbors rather than pillage them.

What is more, as we shall see, we already have many models of what we will call *transformational organizations* for inspiration, organizations as diverse as the U.S. Marine Corps, Alcoholics Anonymous, monasteries the world over, and the IBM Executive School under Louis R. Mobley.

In addition to these organizations that intentionally or consciously offer a transformative experience, many small entrepreneurial companies owe much of their success to "accidentally" offering people transformative experiences, experiences that transcend the stock option plan and all the other motivational levers managers usually rely on to create passion.

What distinguishes the intentional transformational organization from the accidental, however, is endurance. The Marines, Alcoholics Anonymous, and the monastic tradition have all been spectacularly successful for so long precisely because they not only incorporate personal transformation into their missions but institutionalize this process through methodologies such as boot camp, the Twelve Step program, the Rule of St. Benedict, and the 12-week experiential learning program of Mobley's IBM Executive School.

Unfortunately most entrepreneurial start-ups don't realize how much their success depends on offering people the opportunity to be transformed. They fail to institutionalize this impulse through mission and methodology. As a result young companies often lose the spark of innovative passion as they grow, and the corporate training that follows later fails to rekindle it.

If we want the passionate power of the human urge to transformation, then it must be clearly articulated and methodologically institutionalized. If we are to create superior organizations capable of overcoming the myriad problems we face today, then we must tap into the massive amount of human potential that lies dormant in most of our enterprises. And to awaken and harness this potential, we must first understand what people really want from life generally and from the workplace in particular.

But before we begin, let us walk side by side with Brother Robert for a little way. Philosophically this book argues that despite all the relativistic notions that are now so fashionable, the purpose of life is not a matter of opinion or individual taste. This book—dare I say it—*dogmatically* insists that the purpose of every human life, whether we realize it or not, is to be transformed from a selfish into a selfless person. The monk's last prayer each night at Compline is for a restful night and a peaceful death. This book is my prayer that by learning to live like a Trappist, we may all be granted the grace to die like one as well.

WHAT WE
ALL REALLY WANT

All religions then, seek a "summit" of holiness,
of experience, of inner transformation to which their
believers—or an elite of believers—aspire because they
hope, so to speak, to incarnate in their own lives the
highest values in which they believe. To put it in grossly
oversimplified language, all religions aspire to a "union
with God" in some way or another.
—*Thomas Merton*

EMPLOYEE ENGAGEMENT is one of those buzz terms that keeps business pundits busy. And for good reason: the more engaged people are, the more productive they are, and the entire organization benefits. Employee engagement is actually just a newfangled term for what used to be called "corporate loyalty," and, unfortunately for productivity, employees are reporting decreasing levels of this intangible but critically important asset.

Since 1985 the Kenexa High Performance Institute has been compiling its WorkTrends report on employee engagement by asking employees how closely they agree with the following statements:

1. I am proud to tell people I work for my organization.
2. Overall, I am extremely satisfied with my organization as a place to work.
3. I would gladly refer a good friend or family member to my organization for employment.
4. I rarely think about looking for a new job with another organization.

According to the most recent WorkTrends report:

> 2011 was a year of declining levels of employee engagement.
> While some declines were noted in 2010, the pace and spread
> of decline heightened in 2011. The phenomena of declining
> employee engagement was not limited in geographic scope,
> job type, or even industry.

Today's corporate warriors are looking for something more—
much more—from their work, something that transcends the usual
motivational levers of more money and bigger job titles. As we saw
in the preceding chapter, the remarkable economic success of Mepkin Abbey and of Trappist monasteries all over the world relies in
large part on the passionate "engagement" of men like Father Malachy. I believe we can reverse the tide of employee disengagement
by applying the monastic model to our secular organizations. But
to do so, we must first answer the question, What do we really
want from life and, more specifically, from our work?

◯

I WAS SITTING in Father Christian's small office at Mepkin Abbey. I
was early for our appointment, but, just as I expected, he soon
burst in. He greeted me warmly, and I marveled once more at the
vitality of this lithe ninety-year-old man. Under his arm were a
couple of books, one obviously a textbook. Curious, I asked about
it, and I was amazed to find it was a textbook on quantum theory.
He said that, much to his embarrassment, his knowledge of physics was decidedly "anachronistic," and he considered it high time
to "bone up" by solitarily working his way through this impossible-
looking book.

As he filled me in on his progress, I thought about the mystery
surrounding this man. I just couldn't hold the contradictions together in my mind. On the one hand, Father Christian is one of the

most sophisticated, even urbane, human beings I have ever met. He hails from a wealthy family in Washington, DC, and is as comfortable discussing the relative merits of exclusive New England boarding schools as he is discussing the weather. He has PhDs in philosophy, theology, and canon law and was already a successful lawyer when he decided to become a Franciscan priest. He has a prodigious memory and peppers his points with quotations from Shakespeare, Gerard Manley Hopkins, and a host of other authors and poets, and as he does so, he moves effortlessly among English, French, Latin, and Greek as his source demands. He ceaselessly reads St. Thomas Aquinas's *Summa Theologica* in the original Latin, and he told me almost sternly one time: "Listen, if you want to get *anywhere* spiritually, you must be *soaked* in St. Thomas." On the other hand, he is the epitome of the silent, contemplative, Trappist monk. No one is more stringently dedicated to the letter of the Rule of St. Benedict. I once asked if he ever fell asleep between the predawn services of Vigils and Lauds, when by rights monks and monastic guests like me were all in our rooms engaged in either meditation or the discipline of Lectio Divina—the slow, methodical, mindful reading of sacred scripture. The searching way he scanned my face left no doubt he had divined the motive behind my question. Then he growled, "Now I won't say I've never closed my eyes in all these years, but you could count them on one hand. Remember, to God go the first fruits." Striding away, he felt compelled to clear up any lingering ambiguity by looking over his shoulder and emphatically repeating, "the *first* fruits."

Ascetic in his habits, he eats next to nothing, is as lean as a famine year, and avoids the high-octane coffee that seems to fuel the monastery. In all the years I've been going to Mepkin Abbey, I have never known him to miss one of the eight communal services that make up the monastic day. After the last service before retiring, Compline, you will find him in the chapel kneeling deep in prayer.

He never leaves the monastery, as his vow of "stability" precludes it, and even at ninety he remembers St. Benedict's admonition to physical labor. We once teamed up on one of the monastery's most exacting tasks—cleaning out the chicken coops. We extracted hundreds of the monastery's shrieking hens from their cages as they defecated all over us both in protest. He is punctual to a fault and once, in order to be on time, ran the almost half mile from the cloister to a meeting with a group of retreatants I had brought to the monastery.

As he wound up his short lecture on quantum mechanics, my curiosity boiled over, and I decided to risk rebuff by asking a deeply personal question. Why had a man of his omnivorous interests, talents, love of learning, people, and most of all conversation, decided to become a silent contemplative in one of the strictest monasteries in the strictest order of the Catholic Church?

"I made a mistake!" he fairly shouted. Then his amazing blue eyes screwed closed, his chin fell to his chest, and he doubled up with laughter while beating a musical tattoo on the arms of his chair. He laughed so long and hard that when he finally stopped, there were a few faint flecks of spittle glistening in his long, gray beard until he wiped them away with a handkerchief. He told me that after years as a Franciscan, he had visited a Trappist monastery in Canada, from curiosity. "I was taking the tour when I made the mistake of asking myself a question. Anyway, after years of wrestling, I finally realized that darn fool question had me pinned. Next thing you know I found myself here."

I asked, "What was the question?"

"What would it be like to give myself totally to God?"

Whether Father Christian was moved by his admission, my reaction, or both, I cannot say. But we sat for a good long time in silence as I gradually regained my composure. Finally he lifted his chin off his chest and opened his eyes. "There's something terribly wrong with spirituality today," he said, sadly pointing at the other book he had brought to our meeting. "It's as though the materialism that has a death grip on this culture has taken our spirituality as well. Most of what's called spiritual is actually humanistic, if you think about it. People don't want the adventure of God on his own terms and for his own sake. They want a better world, a happier life, better relationships, and all the trimmings that go along with it. Most of it isn't spiritual; it's sweetly comforting and sentimental. It's merely edifying." "Merely edifying" sounded like something toxic he was disposing of with 10-foot tongs. "Now don't get me wrong," he continued. "Our Lord meant it when he commanded us to love one another. I spent several years in Uganda as a chaplain, and my experience there remains crucial to my life. I didn't expect those wonderful people to have so much more to give than I did. I learned the spirit of real charity in Uganda. Real *caritas*—charity—means all you have to give is not enough; you long to give more and find tender humility in that fact. What I mean is the way in which modern spirituality makes God the means to an end and not the end itself. We're urged to seek God *because* this or that human good will come of it. People don't realize 'because' implies that the end is the human good and Truth merely the means. Selfishness becomes the false god in this equation. That's why I always turn to the church fathers, the saints, the mystics: people who climb spiritual mountains simply because they're there to be climbed and it's our destiny to climb them. St. Bernard said it best: 'Amo quia amo, amo ut amem.'" Four years of high school Latin failed me, and I looked at him quizzically. "I love because I love, I love in order to love," he translated. "Take Thomas Aquinas, for example." And he lit up with the innocent enthusiasm that the mere mention of his hero always produced.

"He's a doctor of the Church and in the Middle Ages almost single-handedly resurrected Greek philosophy. He was so darn smart, he could keep the thread of five different books he was writing in his head at once. Five clerks took dictation in turn so he wouldn't have to wait while they wrote. The *Summa Theologica*, his masterpiece, is 3,500 pages long, but did you know it's unfinished?"

I shook my head.

"One day he just stopped writing. His secretary kept asking when they would resume work, and he kept sending him away. Finally the fellow got up the courage to ask him what was going on, and Thomas said, 'I've had an experience of God, and I now know that everything I have written is mere straw. I will never write another word.'"

"Every time I pick up a modern book, I'm left wondering, where is the *mysterium tremendum,* the agape, the Fear of the Lord? Where is the power, the wonder, the majesty, the glory, the supernatural, the fear and trembling, the abject awe? Where is the *transcendence?*"

Again we sat in silence.

"I think I know what you mean, Father," I finally said, though I wondered if I ever would. "The difference between a person who has actually experienced transcendence and one who has not must be . . . well . . ."

"Infinite," he said, supplying the word I was groping for. "The difference is *infinite.*"

THE UNITED STATES is the wealthiest and most successful country the world has ever seen. As my mother used to patiently point out whenever we complained, the average American with central heat, flush toilets, a preowned car, and a Novocain-equipped dentist lives better than the kings of England not too long ago. Yet the Dalai Lama has described Americans as the most miserable people on earth. The World Health Organization recently cited depression as the most serious disease afflicting Western countries today, and I recently learned that one in four incoming freshmen at one of our most prestigious universities is already on anti-depressants. Estimates suggest that as many as 40 million Americans struggle with substance abuse; obesity is reaching epidemic proportions;

and our suicide rate exceeds that in many developing countries. Yet to read the news, one would almost think that if we could just get the economy growing again, everything would be fine.

Again, what do we all really want from our lives, careers, and businesses, and why are we having so much trouble finding it?

○

ONE OF THE MOST useful things I learned as a sales and marketing executive is the concept of "dollar votes." Dollar votes is the business corollary of the dictum that what we do reveals far more about what we really want than what we think, feel, or say. A dollar vote argues that if we really want to understand what motivates people, we should look at how people actually spend their money rather than at survey or focus group data. After all, money is just a mechanism for storing human time and energy and making it portable, and as mortal creatures with tightly constricted life spans, how we utilize these scarce resources is the best way to divine our true priorities. I may argue quite persuasively that helping others is my top priority, but if I donate far more money to my favorite casino than to my favorite charity, I shouldn't be surprised if you remain unconvinced.

In my own company, after some disappointing forays with surveys, we dispensed with this type of market research altogether. Instead, whenever we had a new product idea, we would presell the product into our customer base with a discount for prerelease software. Only if our customers were willing to pony up cold, hard cash would we in turn invest in full-blown product development. If the requisite number of sales was not forthcoming, we gave refunds to the disappointed few and headed back to the drawing board. This approach guaranteed that every product we introduced had a market, and it was actually less expensive and time consuming than more traditional forms of market research.

When we look at the world through the lens of dollar votes, we see an almost insatiable human demand for stories. Books, movies, and television are multibillion-dollar industries, and their primary business is storytelling. Even music, like poetry, is primarily the art of storytelling set to melody. The fact that we spend so much money on stories—in good times and bad—demonstrates that stories offer something that we really want, not just something we like to say we want. And what most stories offer is the vicarious experience of transformation.

We all learned in English 101 that in every compelling story, the main character must be transformed over the arc of the story in some essential way. The main character quite literally must be a different person at the end than he was at the beginning, and in the most uplifting examples the main character ends up a wiser and more selfless individual. Even "dark" stories are usually tales of protagonists like Darth Vader from *Star Wars* or Michael Corleone from *The Godfather,* who yield to the selfish side of their nature with disastrous results. These darker stories are as old as Greek tragedy, and they usually serve as cautionary tales of what happens to mere mortals when they try to exalt themselves over gods and men. Characters may be transformed toward the darkness of selfishness or toward the light of selflessness, but the dramatic tension in almost every story is maintained by this transformational arc, one way or the other.

Without this transformational arc, we may have a spectacle, but we don't have a story. According to dollar votes, the fact that we spend so much time and money watching others being transformed proves that it is this essential transformation from selfishness to selflessness that we all really want. Of course the tragic part of this analysis is that for most of us, this urge toward transformation remains vicarious, and I believe this is the reason why we often feel a bit of a letdown after even the most inspiring stories. Somewhere deep inside, we realize that just as we can't pay someone else to go to the gym, we can't be transformed secondhand, either.

The Hero's Journey

IN RECENT YEARS movies such as *The Matrix, The Truman Show, Star Wars, Groundhog Day, Avatar,* and *The Devil Wears Prada* have brought in billions at the box office. What few realize is that many of these films and a host of others are intentionally based on Joseph Campbell's seminal work *The Hero with a Thousand Faces.* Campbell spent a lifetime researching myths, folktales, and the world's religious traditions only to find that while there are many surface distinctions, the theme of the hero's transformative journey is repeated like clockwork. Many famous filmmakers, such as George Lucas and Steven Spielberg, have drawn from Campbell's work, and even films that don't intentionally follow Campbell's formula often do so by default; after all, Campbell was simply articulating the heroic theme that has been powering storytelling for millennia.

Again, by applying our concept of dollar votes, the fact that we find films based on the Hero's Journey so irresistible demonstrates that transformation, or what Father Christian called transcendence, is what we all really want and what is so painfully missing from our lives. And if we want the same kind of employee engagement and customer loyalty in our secular organizations that we see at Mepkin Abbey, then we must offer people the opportunity to satisfy this hunger for transformation.

While Campbell outlines many stages on the Hero's Journey, these are the major ones:

1. The Call
2. Resistance to the Call
3. The Desert
4. The Great Trial
5. Death and Rebirth
6. Return to Help Others

The Call

The Call, or what the monks call *vocation,* is the invitational stage
of the Hero's Journey. Whether it is through Father Christian asking his "darn fool question" or Morpheus in *The Matrix* offering
Neo the chance to see "how deep this rabbit hole goes," the hero is
invited to abandon the beaten path of business as usual in exchange for adventure and, ultimately, self-transcendence.

In business the Call can take a variety of forms, from the unexpected offer of a new and more challenging position to the chance
to go back to school for an MBA to that mysterious voice that
calls incessantly to every future entrepreneur.

Resistance to the Call

In the monastic tradition, the second stage, Resistance to the Call,
is called *discernment* and corresponds to the lengthy incubation
period that Father Christian spent wrestling with his question. In
cinema it is often represented by the hero's initially hostile reaction to the idea that he come "out of retirement" for "one last mission." In business Resistance to the Call takes place in the soul
searching and "due diligence" we all go through before changing
careers, taking a longed-for sabbatical, starting our own company,
or even asking the boss for a raise. A company considering a fundamental change to its business model goes through an intense
period of "discernment" before taking the leap.

The Desert

Whenever a monk dies, a "holy card" with his photo is issued.
Below his dates of birth and death is the date when he "entered" the
monastic life as a postulant. "Entering" is a monk's second birth-

day and marks the beginning of the third stage of the Hero's Journey: the Desert. This is the "ascetic" stage, when the hero, usually with the help of a teacher, mentor, or just old-fashioned adversity, goes through an arduous process of training and personal development. In the monastic tradition, the Desert is where a monk is "formed" through a process of intellectual, moral, psychological, and spiritual development known as *formation*.

The word *asceticism* is actually derived from the Greek for athletic training, and it is this wider, nonreligious sense of the word that is applicable to many cinematic dramatizations, such as *The Devil Wears Prada*, which are secular in nature and only metaphorically spiritual. The Desert stage may last for years, and since it is often marked by little more than monotonous tenacity in the face of continual failure orchestrated by a well-intentioned but exasperating teacher, it is not surprising that its cinematic depictions are usually radically abbreviated.

In *The Devil Wears Prada*, for example, the Desert is depicted through a montage of an unending series of coats flying each morning from Meryl Streep's character onto the desk of Anne Hathaway's character and into her face—a montage that cleverly suggests the passage of time as well as the frustration that all great teachers, from Yoda in *Star Wars* to Father Christian, inspire as they insist on only our best.

In business the Desert is the phase of intense struggle as we try to master a new job or an entire new set of skills while feeling like we are "playing way over our heads" most of the time. What makes the Desert even more challenging is that, like taking golf lessons, it usually involves a regressive stage: things initially get worse before they get better. J.C. Penney is currently in the Desert. At least temporarily the new CEO's efforts to transform the business model by weaning customers off discounts has led to a regressive fall-off in revenue as the company struggles to reinvent itself. Similarly, it is the exceedingly rare entrepreneur who doesn't spend many a sleepless night in the Desert wondering why he traded a "perfectly good job" for the "unholy hell" of the regressive stage of entrepreneurship. (I certainly did.)

The Great Trial

The fourth stage of the Hero's Journey is the Great Trial: the hero is tempted to use the power built up through his training in the Desert for selfish rather than selfless purposes. In movie after movie, dramatic tension is produced by uncertainty as we wonder whether the hero will overcome temptation or be seduced, like Darth Vader, by the Dark Side of selfishness. The devil tempts Jesus with selfish power in the desert, and it is power that Meryl Streep's character eventually offers Anne Hathaway's character in *The Devil Wears Prada*.

In the monastic tradition, the Great Trial is often referred to as the Dark Night of the Soul; the psychological crisis that often precedes spiritual surrender.

In recent years a number of onetime financial superstars, such as Bernie Madoff, have gone to prison because when confronted with the Great Trial of facing their own limitations, they succumbed instead to the temptation of illicitly gained power and prestige. Another example of the Great Trial in business is often described as "hitting the wall." A career stalls, and all the "skills" and personal power accumulated in the Desert no longer seem to work. It is axiomatic in business that when this happens, it is usually because our aspiring corporate hero has failed to learn that every business is a people business. In a selfish rush for the upper rungs of the corporate ladder, he has made too many enemies, failed to share credit, and been typecast as the kind of "I, me, and miner" who is all take and no give. Intent on being the smartest person in the room, he doesn't know what it means to "take one for the team." Hitting the wall for selfish reasons is so common in corporate America that our most prestigious business schools are often lambasted by successful executives for overemphasizing "hard skills" at the expense of the "soft people values" that are so typical of the monks and so critical to their success.

Death and Rebirth

The climax of the Hero's Journey is Death and Rebirth. The hero has gone as far as he can under his own power, realizes the folly of selfishness, reaches out for help, and surrenders to "grace," either literally or, more often, metaphorically, in the form of love.

In *The Matrix*, despite the power accrued in the Desert under the tutelage of Morpheus, Neo cannot overcome his Great Trial, Agent Smith, on his own. He dies, only to be brought back to life by the love of a woman. This woman, who just happens to be named Trinity, offers a lifeline of grace symbolically represented by a phone line to the hero mired in the illusion of the Matrix. This phone line metaphorically connects the "heaven" of the real world, where Trinity resides, to the "earth" of the illusory Matrix.

In the monastic tradition, death and rebirth are symbolically re-enacted through Solemn Profession, when, after years in the Desert as a novice, the monk takes his final vows. The monk "dies to the world" and is "reborn" as a full-fledged member of the community. Whatever the plot line, the Death and Rebirth stage marks the transformation of the hero. An inner alchemy takes place, and the hero is radically transformed. The aspiring monk is never offered Solemn Profession unless in the eyes of the abbot, the novice master, and the community at large, this transformation has taken place.

In business, as in its cinematic representations, Death and Rebirth is a scary and often painful process. In our previous example, people who have hit the wall in their career usually tenaciously resist "surrendering" the selfish habits and individual ambition that worked so well in the past. Showing vulnerability, admitting mistakes, helping others, and being open are so unnatural and frightening that, like Bill Murray's character in *Groundhog Day,* they find ceaselessly repeating the same mistakes a more palatable alternative. But, again like Murray's character, they may experience a "breakthrough." Through the helping hand of a loving spouse, friend, or mentor—or just a confluence of circumstances—our corporate hero may face his limitations, admit selfish mistakes, and open up to others. He "dies" and is "reborn," and when he does, his stalled career usually takes off.

Return to Help Others

The hero is now ready to embark on the final stage, the Return to Help Others. This stage is particularly well portrayed in the final scene of *The Devil Wears Prada*. First Anne Hathaway's character gives away all the expensive clothes she got in Paris. This symbolizes her monkish "renunciation" of her "old life" and its selfish priorities. Giving up her clothing also symbolizes renouncing the body or "flesh," which is also a well-worn monastic metaphor for renouncing selfishness. The monk trades in his street clothes for a habit and a vow of poverty.

Next she meets her teacher one last time, and though she is initially rejected, the little smile she gets from Meryl Streep's character in her limo suggests that she has transcended her need for a teacher and become a teacher herself. In the final scene, Anne Hathaway's character is radiantly walking up the street, at peace with herself and the world. She has become the business version of Buddhism's compassionate bodhisattva, on her way to help others on their journey toward transformation.

One of the most important rules from St. Benedict is that monks must offer hospitality to any sojourner, wayfarer, or pilgrim who comes to the monastery looking for shelter. It is through hospitality that the Return to Help Others finds its place in the monastic tradition. The demand for Father Christian's spiritual direction from people like me is bottomless, but I've never known him to turn anyone away. And it is this open-handed hospitality in the service of others that is critical to monastic business success.

Similarly, the transformed businessperson—or business—offers monastic hospitality through selfless service toward colleagues, customers, stockholders, and stakeholders. Paradoxically, now that climbing the corporate ladder is no longer so important, our transformed corporate hero usually starts taking three rungs at a time.

The Hero's Journey can be abbreviated even further than my truncated summary of Campbell's work would suggest. Regardless of how many stages we delineate or whether it is portrayed as religious or secular, Campbell's model is always a transformational journey from selfishness to selflessness.

The Three Kinds of Transformation

LIFE ITSELF can actually be described as a longing for transformation. Every acorn longs to become an oak, and life itself is a transformational journey from life to death and back to life again. Abraham Maslow's famous hierarchy of human needs is an incredible insight into human motivation, but his model can be described as well in terms of a longing for transformation.

Although all human motivation arises from a longing for transformation, there are three different types of transformation. When a thirsty man drinks, he transforms his *condition*. When a poor man hits the lottery, he transforms his *circumstance*. And when Mr. Scrooge wakes up on Christmas morning an utterly new man, he has experienced a transformation of *being*.

All three types of transformation are necessary. It is only when we try to replace one type of transformation with another that we get into trouble. When we turn sustenance into "comfort food," we are actually trying to fill that hole in our soul by overfilling our stomach. Comfort food is an attempt to substitute a transformation of condition for a transformation of being, often with disastrous results. Food, drugs, alcohol, and sex produce transformations of condition, and when used properly, all have their place. It is only when we mistakenly use them as a substitute for a transformation of being that things go terribly awry. The ecstatic "rush" of drugs may feel like self-transcendence, but as every addict ultimately finds out, it is merely the gateway to hell.

Power and fame are transformations of circumstance, and they, too, have their place. Self-determination relies on a modicum of power, and we all need a bit of fame, in the form of recognition, to live a fruitful life. The lust for unbridled power, however, rests on the erroneous assumption that if we can force people to treat us differently, this will somehow transform us. Fame relies on a similar error: if we can transform people's opinion, this will somehow transform us. Eventually the truth sets in that no matter how famous or powerful we become, we are still the same person we always were, and the feeling of hypocrisy—combined with the enormous amount of psychic energy it takes to maintain the pretense—is the reason why so many celebrities self-destruct and so many powerful people are "wrecked by success."

So much of the emptiness and ennui that we feel individually and collectively is the result of trying to substitute a transformation of condition and/or circumstance for the transformation of being that we really want. In business, however, we are taught that every problem represents an opportunity.

Recently business books such as *Megatrends 2010* have argued that spirituality will be the defining business trend of the twenty-first century. I would argue that the universal appeal of movies based on Campbell's model demonstrate that this trend is already well under way. For the first time in human history, economic conditions have made the Hero's Journey possible for the many and not just the few. In this reading the depression, social ills, and fall-off in employee engagement I mentioned earlier are not just symptomatic of decadence and decline. Instead they represent a Burning Bush calling us individually and collectively toward something higher and more meaningful than a full stomach and a trophy house. And our suspicion, along with Neo's in *The Matrix*, that there is "something wrong with the world" may only be a well-intentioned teacher calling to our higher nature by frustrating our lower.

It is in this sense that the monastic business model is both ancient and emergent. It is ancient because for more than 1,500 years, it has offered the Hero's Journey to the few. It is emergent because we are finally at the point where the monastic formula can be applied by the many.

Free Cokes in the break room is a great motivational idea but offers only a transformation of condition. Stock options are wonderful as well, but they offer only a transformation of circumstance. In order to duplicate the monastic business success in our secular organizations, we must offer our employees, stakeholders, and even customers the opportunity for the same transformation of being that every heroic figure must attain. Today the most exciting trend in business is the emphasis on authentic leadership and authentic brands, and authenticity means individually and collectively transcending selfishness through a transformation of being.

3

THE END OF SELFISHNESS

I WAS A SOPHOMORE in college in 1972, and through some hustle and sheer luck, I landed four front-row seats to a Rolling Stones concert. We threw a marathon party the night before the sacred event with nothing but Stones music, and when my three friends and I arrived at the concert, we were adorned with body paint and homemade "Sticky Fingers" T-shirts. I was also sporting a red, white, and blue Uncle Sam top hat, recalling the Stones's previous tour, when Mick Jagger had worn a similar hat.

Just before the concert, a roadie strolled to the front of the stage, bent over, and, through a thick British accent, said, "Mick wan's to wea' your 'at." Moments later the Stones were bouncing all over the stage, and Jagger was wearing *my* hat. I was so delirious with joy that I didn't really mind when, during an encore of "Jumpin' Jack Flash," my hat went spinning over my head into the crowd and was promptly torn to pieces. I didn't mind, because Mick Jagger wore *my* hat.

But while we were working our way toward the car after the concert, a funny thing happened. I was disappointed and let down in a way that I couldn't understand. It was a vague sense of "Now what?" or "Where do I go from here?," and it lingered for almost two weeks before gradually dissipating.

At the time I couldn't understand these feelings of profound disappointment, and they made me so anxious that I didn't really try. But I think I understand them now. Watching the Stones from the front row with Mick wearing my hat was supposed to mean something. It was supposed to transform my life, transform me. I was supposed be a new person permanently propelled to a whole new level of existence by the experience.

Instead, as the euphoria wore off, I knew that nothing essential had changed. I was the same old me, wrestling with the same old problems and mundane trivialities, mired in the same old fears and insecurities. After a glimpse of heaven, here I was, back on earth. Worst of all, at just twenty, I sensed through a glass darkly that eager anticipation followed by inevitable disappointment might very well become the pattern of my life.

The Power of Passion

I WAS HAVING LUNCH with one of my clients, the CEO of a rapidly growing midsized company, when I casually asked for his job description.

He smiled and said, "Well, if you followed me around, you'd probably think I do lots of things. But I only have one job. I build passion. Most people think talent is in short supply. Hell, the papers are full of stories about regular folks working miracles when something they really care about is on the line. Talent is not in short supply. Passion is. My job is showing people that what we're doing is worth doing. I provide the whys so our people can provide the hows. Once passion is in place," he said with a big grin, "my job becomes insisting that people use their vacation and trying to stay out of the way."

Louis R. Mobley, my mentor and one of the leaders of the IBM Executive School in the 1950s and 1960s, would certainly agree. He often said that the task of management is creating superior organizations by getting extraordinary results from ordinary people. He argued that leadership is not about getting things done; it is providing a mission worth doing in the first place. "Hell," he would say with a smile, "if we're doing the wrong things, we'd be better off being only half as efficient in getting them done."

Mobley called *mission* the "spirit of the enterprise" and he said that a worthwhile mission, properly articulated, galvanizes ordinary people with extraordinary, even explosive, results. He was so adamant about the importance of mission that he created a *teleocratic,* or "purpose-driven," management model to replace the bureaucratic or "policies and procedures"–driven paradigm that is still so prevalent today.

The 1,500-year-old monastic tradition and the extraordinary business accomplishments of the monks of Mepkin Abbey illustrate the importance of mission—not only to the passion necessary for success, but more importantly to the sustainable success that all organizations crave, whether religious or secular.

As we discussed in chapter 1, what the monastic mission offers to both aspiring monks and the thousands of people who flock to monasteries to share in their lifestyle temporarily is the opportunity for transformation. The monastic tradition survives and monastic businesses thrive because—unlike a Rolling Stones concert—the monastic mission offers an opportunity for a permanent transformative experience, a radical "change of heart" that lifts us out of ourselves and our petty concerns through a teleocratic management model that I am calling *service and selflessness.*

Whether we realize it or not, a permanent transformation of being is ultimately what we all really want, and this transformation of being, whether personal or organizational, is a transformation from selfishness to selflessness. This longing for transformation is so basic to human nature that when organizations tap into it through mission and methodology, people respond with the same passionate zeal and "prayerful attitude" toward their work that lies at the heart of monastic business success.

While it may seem like we want an easy life of self-indulgence and immediate gratification, if we look a little closer, we would probably admit that we are most satisfied when we are selflessly sacrificing for something eminently worthwhile. We all too often act as if happiness lies in realizing our selfish desires, but most of our free time is spent trying to "forget ourselves" and "lose ourselves" in distraction or daydreaming. The English language is also full of phrases like "lost in thought" or "absorbed in a task" that illustrate our longing for selflessness.

On the other hand, our associations with the term "self-conscious" are all negatively charged. We associate self-consciousness with stage fright or the feeling of not being able to "get with it" or "out of our own way." Nothing ruins a party, a movie, a speech, a golf swing, or making love faster than finding ourselves self-consciously unable to "lose" or "forget" ourselves in the activity. This selfish sense of self is so painful that modern life is often described as a relentless search for selfless or "mindless" distraction. And distraction, by definition, is something we "lose ourselves" in so we can "forget ourselves." But the problem with distraction is that it is as fleeting and impermanent as a Rolling Stones concert. Sooner or later we "come back to ourselves" with a sense of loss and nameless regret. This is why an endless search for distraction so often leads to increasing ennui and the depressing sense that the "world is too much with us." It is not the world that is too much with us, but ourselves.

The pain of self-consciousness and our search for new and ever more elusive forms of distraction illustrates that it is selflessness, not selfishness, that we all really want. Distraction, momentarily at least, transforms us from selfish to selfless people.

We are happiest and most productive when our sense of time disappears and we are oblivious of ourselves. This is not a state of unconsciousness. It is that highly coveted state of spontaneity, when every shot finds the hoop and every sales call results in a sale. The magic of spontaneity demonstrates yet again that deep down, we long for an "escape" from the prison of selfishness. What we are really longing for is a permanent transformation of being from self-ishness to selflessness—that permanent, effortless state of spontaneity that artists, Trappist monks, and Zen masters labor so hard to describe. What we want is a mission so good, pure, and mission-critical that we would selflessly "lose ourselves" in it and "give ourselves away" to it passionately, utterly, spontaneously, and without reservation. And any organization, like Mepkin Abbey, full of passionate people selflessly and spontaneously serving a worthwhile mission is bound to be fabulously successful.

Service and Selflessness: A Corporate Case Study

MY FIRST TEACHER, a West Virginia hillbilly and Zen master, often said that reaping the benefits of service and selflessness meant mastering the "habit of becoming accident-prone." In deference to the delicate sensibilities of my actuarial friends in the insurance industry, I use the term "happy accidents" instead. And it was a happy accident brought about by aiming past the target that landed me a gig several years ago at New York City–based Yext Corporation. Though Yext has since expanded into other businesses, at the time it was focused exclusively on the exploding field of Internet-driven, performance-based advertising.

I had the unique opportunity of working for MTV when it launched in 1981, and the Yext corporate culture had the same look and feel. The CEO and president, fresh off two previous successful start-ups, were both pushing the ripe old age of twenty-eight. The 60 or so employees were even younger—most just out of college. Crammed into bare-bones, warehouse-like office space with oak beam floors, the company was barely two years old, was growing exponentially, and had that gonzo energy that brought back so many memories of MTV in its infancy and my own stint as an entrepreneur.

Jim Collins, my boss and mentor at what is now the A&E Network, once told me, "Augie, when you take a new job, hire somebody, fire somebody, rearrange the furniture . . . but for God's sake make something happen fast." Then he grinned. "And by the way, if what you do makes money, that would be nice, too." Even though I'd been hired as a consultant at Yext, I knew the founders were not the kind of guys who pay for "advice." They were entrepreneurs to their fingernails, and though my marching orders were sketchy (I was supposed to help the company "scale"), I knew I had to make an impact fast without doing anything that would derail all the great momentum the company already had going.

Most of Yext's employees were sales reps signing up small businesses over the phone, and within days I commandeered the conference room to run a number of tests on some ideas I had for boosting revenue, setting goals, and scaling the sales force. The president lent me four sales reps for these tests, including the company superstar, a young man named Alan. But despite my bringing all the charm I could muster, Alan and I crossed swords almost immediately.

No one dislikes price increases, change in the pitch, change in the sales model, spare change, or change, period, more than a salesman. And no salesman I ever knew pushed back harder than Alan. He was arrogant, stubborn, and downright uncoachable, and his impatient selling style was rude, pushy, patronizing, and abusive toward clients. He reminded me of the old adage about generals: whatever cannot be achieved with force can always be achieved with more force.

After a particularly trying day, I finally mentioned my difficulties to the president. He just smiled and told me to forget about it. Alan was a son of a bitch, but he was "our son of a bitch." He was cordially disliked and going nowhere in the company, but as long as he kept putting up big numbers, it was company policy to work around him. So that's what I tried to do.

Despite Alan's resistance, one of the things that emerged from the tests was a possible new revenue stream for the company. Performance-based advertising meant that unlike with the Yellow Pages or other traditional advertising models, Yext's customer base of tens of thousands of small businesses only paid a fee when they actually got a qualified phone call from a new customer. Yext tracked these phone calls to everything from auto repair shops to podiatrists to veterinarians, and only when a call was successful was the client's credit card billed.

Yet Yext offered many ancillary services free of charge, and our tests strongly suggested that customers would willingly pay a monthly fee for these services. Like a cable television bill, a monthly fee would provide a recurring revenue stream to complement the company's existing model of variable sales. Besides, there is nothing like recurring revenue to juice Wall Street for an eventual IPO.

Two weeks after arriving at Yext, I presented my test results to the CEO and the president late on a Friday afternoon. On Monday morning I was aghast to find that over the weekend, all the billing codes had been put in place, a newsletter had been sent to the customer base, the switch had been flipped, thousands of credit cards had been hit, and hundreds of thousands of dollars of recurring revenue was cascading into the bank account on its way straight to the bottom line.

"My God," I blurted, "couldn't we have tested five hundred or so to make sure that half the customer base doesn't spit the bit?" Enjoying my horrified reaction to their bad-boy prank, they both laughed and told me to relax: they knew their customers, and there would be few, if any, defections. Within hours it was clear they were right. But I didn't relax. In fact, my anxiety increased.

I've worked in dozens of corporations over the years and started a couple myself. If there is any truth to the Dilbert mythology that martinet managers bark orders as cowering employees jump to comply, I have yet to see it. What really had me worried was not the existing customers but the sales force. Flipping the switch on current customers is one thing, but getting 50 sales reps right out of college to charge a monthly fee for something they've always given away for free is quite another. To make matters worse, there were no plans to raise commissions or lower sales quotas based on this new selling challenge.

I knew that if the sales reps dug in their heels and went "on strike" over the new fee and sales production went off a cliff as a result, it would be the fee—and, by extension, me—that would bear the blame. Nothing was more important to the company than sales velocity, and no matter how juicy the fee revenue might be, it would not survive a full-blown sales force revolt.

I hastily put together a rollout plan for the implementation and volunteered to retrain the sales force myself. As I expected, my arguments for the fee were met with ominous skepticism and a still more ominous silence. Things got so tense during the third or fourth training session that I made a mistake. I cut off a young sales rep named Amy in mid-sentence with a mild rebuke for being "negative."

At the time I didn't give it a thought, but the next morning Amy gave me the cold shoulder. I felt terrible about it. I tried a couple of times to speak to her but she adamantly insisted that there was "nothing" wrong. When I mentioned it to the president and the vice president of sales, they both passed it off with a "she'll get over it," but it still bothered me.

Coming back from yet another training session, I passed by Alan's desk. Without thinking, I asked if I could talk with him privately. I told him I really needed his help. I told him about what had happened between me and Amy and how badly I felt about it. Since she was on his team, I asked if he would be willing to intercede for me. Would he tell her how much I liked her and how sorry I was?

Suddenly his eyes widened, the tense lines on his forehead relaxed, and he broke into a boyish grin that I didn't know he had.

Clapping me soundly on the shoulder, he exclaimed: "Don't worry, Aug, I got your back!" First thing next morning, Amy greeted me warmly, and 30 minutes later, I was offering Alan a big barrel of pretzels along with a handwritten note expressing my gratitude.

The very next day Alan walked into my office and asked to speak to me. To my surprise he told me that he realized how selfish and difficult he was. It was not just business, he said. His whole life was a mess. As his blue eyes filled with tears, he told me he knew he had to change but didn't know how. He asked if I would help him. Even though we were both putting in very long days, I immediately agreed, and we began secretly meeting in the evenings for coaching sessions.

One week later the sales force started selling the new fee. We put some cash incentives in place, and the first few fees were sold-in without incident. Starting to relax, I had just retreated to my office to answer a few e-mails when an ear-splitting shriek sent me rushing to my door. Looking out over a sea of heads in the vast sales "pit," I was just in time to see a young woman jump to her feet, throw down her headphones, and tell everyone within shouting distance that she had just lost a big sale she had been working for months because of "Augie's damn fee."

Everyone froze, and the atmosphere was so tense you could have hung an axe on it. Thirty years of experience told me that things were going south very quickly. I knew I had to move fast to turn things around, but thirty years of experience failed me. I was paralyzed. Suddenly, out of nowhere, Alan appeared. He spoke briefly with the irate rep, but I was too far away to hear what was said. Then he sat down at her desk, picked up her headphones, and re-called her prospect. Several minutes later the deal was done, and it included "Augie's damn fee." Then he got up, flashed her that same smile that had beguiled me, gave her a hug, and humbly made his way back to his desk on the far side of the sales floor.

Instantly, like a stalled subway suddenly powering up in a tunnel, everyone went back to work. Alan didn't know I was watching, but his act of selfless service not only rescued a sale and a tense situation but ended once and for all the resistance in the sales force. Alan quite literally made his company millions in the space of a few minutes through a selfless gesture, and I felt so strongly about it that the first thing I did when I finally got my heart rate under control was write an e-mail saying as much to the president and CEO and copying Alan. This twenty-four-year-old kid whom I was convinced just a few weeks earlier was "uncoachable" had just saved my behind.

A couple of months later, my contract was up and it was time to go home. A party was held on a weeknight, and I was thrilled when everyone came. Many of the reps told me privately what a difference I'd made in their lives, and that meant the world to me. But the high point of the evening was just sitting with Alan. By now his boyish grin had become a fixed asset for Yext, and for an hour or more, we swapped old war stories about butting heads when I first came on board. After Alan and I hugged and said our goodbyes, the president took me by the arm and pulled me aside. "I was passing Alan's desk today," he said, "and his screen saver is a photo of you. I asked what that was all about, and he said, 'I want Augie in front of me all the time as an inspiration for the kind of person I want to be someday.' "

A couple of months later, I got a phone call from Yext. They had just sold a chunk of the company to some venture capitalists at a monster valuation. During the course of this conversation, I learned that the more-than-generous grant of stock I'd received for my efforts had just appreciated more than 600 percent.

○

NONE OF THIS was part of any plan. I never expected to tap into one young man's longing for transformation with such dramatic results. In fact it was only several months after returning from

New York that the service and selflessness lessons of my experience at Yext gradually dawned on me. Besides the financial benefit, Yext got a much more effective sales rep and an employee who has already been promoted and is slated for more. Podiatrists are getting new patients, sore feet are being soothed, and perhaps a dog or two has been spared a kick or two from a footsore owner. The ripple effects of service and selflessness are potentially endless.

The first monastic lesson here is always *aim past the target*. My volunteer work with college students put me "in play" in a way I could never have possibly expected. Two executives at Yext were former students, and this "happy accident" led to my opportunity with the company.

The second lesson is doing all we do with a monk's "prayerful attitude." It would have been easy to "work around" Alan and wait for Amy to "get over it," but, regardless of what others thought, Yext deserved my best, and I just couldn't let it go.

Third, service and selflessness must become habitual, automatic, and second nature. I still don't know what made me impulsively ask Alan for his help, and like a great salesman making the pitch of his life, I was amazed at the time to hear what was coming out of my mouth.

The fourth secret is *going first*. By humbling myself to Alan, I turned the power equation around by offering fifty-seven-year-old vulnerability to a twenty-four-year-old in his first job. This in turn gave him the room he needed to expose his vulnerability. I was able to reach him through this gesture of trust in a way that no amount of logic, with or without threats, could ever have done. To get "coachability" I had to offer it first. Whatever we want from others, we must have the courage to offer first.

The fifth lesson is having enough faith to "trust the process." There was no guarantee that Alan would react as he did. All my previous experience with him suggested quite the opposite. In fact I was taking quite a risk. It was still very early in my tenure at Yext, and if Alan had rejected me, he could easily have spread it around the company that "this so-called, high-priced 'expert' needed my help just getting along with a twenty-three-year-old girl."

Authenticity and sincerity is the sixth lesson. Despite our head-butting, I really did care about Alan. I took our failure to get along personally, and deep down I saw it as a failure on my part, not his. The same was true with Amy. I honestly felt terrible and was motivated by little more than a sincere desire to make amends.

The seventh lesson is admitting our mistakes. I made a mistake with Amy and owned up to it despite the advice I received to the contrary. The corollary is that every problem is in fact an opportunity. In retrospect, my difficulties with Amy played a pivotal role in what eventually transpired.

Finally, if we stick to our mission of service and selflessness, the monetary and other rewards will take care of themselves. Somewhere along the line, with the help of the monks of Mepkin, I was transformed into someone who now gets most of his kicks out of seeing others succeed. And it seems like the less I worry about money, the more money I make.

The devil is in the details. This is especially true when it comes to making the transformational power of service and selflessness work in a corporate setting. In this case study, a simple gesture offered selflessly to a single person meant millions of dollars right to the bottom line.

4

GOAT RODEOS AND
THE TRANSFORMATIONAL
ORGANIZATION

IN THE MID-1990S I spent a lot of time wandering around Microsoft's corporate campus in Redmond, Washington, developing the strategic alliance that played such a critical role in my own company's success. I always looked forward to these forays—and not merely for the Cherry Coke, which was still unavailable back east, in the break rooms. It was because every Microsoftie I met was breathing fire for Microsoft and its mission. Ten minutes on campus made me feel ten years younger. It reminded me of an even earlier time when I was breathing a similar collective fire for a brash young start-up about to launch MTV: Music Television.

Like children eagerly abandoning their cozy beds for a sleepout, the employees at Microsoft were sleeping under their desks—apparently just for the sheer adventure of it. I was so fascinated by the half-crazed culture fueling Microsoft's fabulous growth that one day I asked a particularly fervent adherent of this secular religion for the secret.

"Goat rodeos!" he shouted in my face.

"What's a *goat rodeo?*" I asked, suddenly feeling our age disparity.

"Bill Gates calls at six o'clock on Friday night. He wants to demo your product at a Tokyo trade show Monday morning for 10,000 people. The product's half done and buggy as hell, but you and your team work like maniacs all weekend, and somehow, you get him the bits. Bill walks out onstage and knocks 'em dead."

"That's *one* goat rodeo," he continued, in a still higher pitch and with ever-gathering ferocity. "And when you've done four or five goat rodeos, you've made your bones at Microsoft."

While I admit that I lack his gift for language, I would argue that what he so colorfully described as a goat rodeo is what we have been calling an opportunity for transformation. The real secret to Microsoft's explosive growth was that Bill Gates and his executive team managed to connect their corporate mission to these transformational experiences. Microsoft's stock produced so many employee millionaires that eventually the term "Microsoft millionaire" was freely bandied about in the press, but I can't recall a single person, during dozens of trips over several years, ever mentioning money. I am not arguing that money (or Cherry Coke) doesn't matter, just that mission and the opportunity to be transformed through serving that mission matters so much more.

That Bill Gates realized it is highly doubtful, but the secret to Microsoft's early success was that it was, at least for a time, what we are calling a *transformational organization.*

The Two Kinds of Transformational Organizations

AS WE NOTED BEFORE, there are two kinds of transformational organizations. Monasteries, Alcoholics Anonymous (AA), the Marine Corps, and the IBM Executive School as led by Louis Mobley are consciously transformational because they clearly articulate a transformation of being, right up front as part of their mission.

Many start-ups, on the other hand, are unconsciously transformational because—like Microsoft in its early years—they accidentally offer transformational opportunities without management clearly articulating this or corporate stakeholders clearly understanding it. I seriously doubt, for example, that goat rodeos were ever mentioned in Microsoft's mission statement or employee handbook. But whether consciously or unconsciously, what all transformational organizations share is a goat-rodeo, gonzo culture that is the real secret to their success.

Yet the problem with unconsciously transformational organizations is that this goat-rodeo mentality fades as the organization grows. Google, for example, tried to combat mass defections through across-the-board bonuses and salary bumps. But while I'm always happy to see people make more money, I will be surprised if money alone has much effect on defections. In the last chapter, we met Yext Corporation. Yext is full of Google defectors, and not a single one left Google for monetary reasons. In fact, they are working far harder and for less money. They left because Google had become staid and boring. They no longer felt the same intimate relationship with Google's mission that used to bring out their best in the fervent belief that they were "making a difference." They left because Google was no longer offering goat rodeos.

In a press release, Google said they were offering money because this is what surveys said employees wanted. I would offer this as an example of what's wrong with surveys. As I noted earlier, the reason why we dispensed with surveys in favor of dollar votes in our own company is because what people say they want and what they really want is so often quite different. My guess is that Google folks didn't really know what was missing and defaulted to money. If I am correct, Google is now in danger of ending up with employees that stick around for the wrong reasons.

When we look at consciously transformational organizations such as monasteries, the Marine Corps, or AA, we find fanatically committed people who, despite widely disparate missions, often evince an almost total disregard for the traditional levers that leaders rely on for producing passionate employee engagement. Monks take a vow of poverty. AA is a completely self-managing, bottom-up organization staffed by volunteers who don't seek recognition but insist on anonymity instead. No one joins the Marines for the money or individual acknowledgment. They join for the opportunity to be part of something far bigger than themselves.

Unlike ads for other branches of the armed services, ads for the Marine Corps never offer transformations of circumstance, things like educational benefits, training for a future career, or even a chance to "see the world." The Marine Corps offers only the opportunity to be one of "the few, the proud, the Marines." Yet the Marines is the only service branch that, even in a time of war, consistently exceeds its recruiting targets. In business, we all know that the best form of marketing is word of mouth, and no word of mouth can compare to tens of thousands of ex-marines shouting "Semper Fi!" and "Once a Marine, always a Marine!" at anyone within earshot—a word-of-mouth testimonial that has no equivalent from Army and Navy veterans.

Similarly, the adherents of AA's Twelve Step program that I have had the honor to meet are so passionately thankful for their transformation that they describe themselves as "Grateful Alcoholics." They are grateful because without their addiction, they never would have encountered the transformative experience of AA.

This is the power of transformation, and, as we saw in the Microsoft story above, corporate entities can tap into this spirit as well.

In contrast to unconsciously transformational corporate success stories, which are typically short lived, consciously transformational organizations display an amazing ability to thrive over long periods of time. The missions are so compelling that either these organizations attract the leadership talent they need or, as with AA, passionate people invent ways to lead themselves.

The Consciously Transformational Organization

Despite obvious differences relative to their specific missions, all consciously transformational organizations have three things in common:

1. A high, overarching mission worthy of being selflessly served
2. Personal transformation as part of the mission
3. A methodology for bringing transformation about

The mission of the Marines, for example, is to serve the country, the Corps, and fellow marines. Monks serve God, their community, and their fellow man. The paradox at the heart of AA's mission is that the best way to stay clean and sober is to selflessly help others stay clean and sober. Despite the technological nature of its business, the mission of Mobley's IBM Executive School was to selflessly develop IBM's people and serve its customers.

Next, each of these organizations clearly offers a transformation of being, right up front. You don't learn to be a monk, a marine, a sober human being, a leader, or even a golfer by reading a book or taking a class. You must *become* one.

Finally, whether it is through the Rule of St. Benedict, Marine boot camp, the Twelve Step program, or Mobley's experiential executive school, every consciously transformational organization has a formal methodology for transforming people. A monk enters as a postulant and gradually becomes a monk. A young man or woman joins as a recruit and gradually becomes a marine. Alcoholics Anonymous takes addicts and over time transforms them into recovering alcoholics. Mobley took managers and transformed them into executives.

The interrelationship of these three critical elements common to all consciously transformational organizations is particularly instructive in AA. Most people believe that the mission of AA is to get people off alcohol. And though much of the literature surrounding Alcoholics Anonymous maintains just that, I beg to differ. The mission of AA is to transform people, by means of the Twelve Step program, into selfless individuals who no longer need alcohol. For instance AA uses the term "dry drunk" to describe a person who has physically stopped drinking but has yet to be transformed. Dry drunks are often angry, irritable, selfish, and depressed, and AA considers them at high risk of relapse. At AA transformation is the goal and sobriety is the effect, not the other way around.

If I am correct, this is a perfect example of what we have been describing as *aiming past the target*. Sobriety for AA is the byproduct of a change of heart: a change of heart (or what the monks might call *conversion*) that produces people who consistently put the interests of others ahead of their own. Alcoholics Anonymous demonstrates once again that when we find the courage to seek first the kingdom of selflessness, the rest takes care of itself.

⬭

DESPITE ITS REPUTATION as a consummate "chick flick," I am a huge fan of *The Devil Wears Prada*. One of my favorite scenes is when Anne Hathaway's character is gamely trying to explain to her father what she is doing with her life. Her father has all the typical fatherly concerns. He can't understand why, after trading an opportunity to go to Stanford's Law School for the dream of becoming a journalist in New York, she is a lowly secretary in the fashion industry—an industry that, her father pointedly reminds her, she doesn't even care about.

Again and again Hathaway's character vainly tries to get her father to see that what she is learning, or, more accurately, becoming, is far more important than any job or mere skill set can convey. To put it in slightly more technical language, the reason why the

Hathaway character and her father talk past each other is that she is thinking *process* while he is thinking *content*. She is talking about goat rodeos, while her father is talking about a job description.

Like any good monk, Hathaway's character metaphorically tries to convey to her father that if she first seeks the kingdom of heaven, everything else will fall into place.

Stripped of this spiritual metaphor, what she actually says in the movie is that what she is learning at the feet of her impossibly demanding boss is the life equivalent of a Swiss Army knife. It will enable her to be successful in anything she may decide to do in business or otherwise.

Hathaway's character is not content to be good at a job; she wants to be good at life. She wants to *become* her best in every sense of the word, and this is exactly what transpires.

Physically, she starts out an awkward—even dowdy—young girl. Over the arc of the story, she is transformed into a supremely confident, drop-dead gorgeous woman.

Professionally, she is transformed from a novice scatter-brain who goes to pieces under the slightest pressure into a multitasking superhero: a superhero who eventually beats her boss at her own game by almost supernaturally getting her hands on the newest Harry Potter book before it is even published. Her metamorphosis takes her from being a human caterpillar who can't handle pressure to a human butterfly who thrives on it.

Psychologically, she grows so much that *The Devil Wears Prada* is one of those rare "chick flicks" that doesn't end with a marriage. She outgrows her friends and even her boyfriend, and, sadly, even he must be left behind.

Spiritually, she starts out selfishly seeking personal power and ends up selflessly giving it all away—even down to the very clothes in her closet.

Aristotle said, "We are what we repeatedly do. Excellence, then, is not a choice but a habit." Excellence must become who we are, and this is exactly what happens to Hathaway's character as she successfully navigates the stages of the Hero's Journey. Sadly her longing for this radical transformation is exactly what her father, boyfriend, and friends can't understand.

The toughest part of the Hero's Journey is the Desert stage. The Desert is so challenging that millions of self-help inspirational books are sold each year based on the bogus premise that you can skip all the work the Desert requires by just "following your bliss." In fact there are no shortcuts around this stage—and the difficulties are not always obvious. For Anne Hathaway's character, the toughest part of the Desert is not her implacable boss. It is the alienation and loneliness she must suffer because no one, not even her father, understands what she is doing and why she is doing it.

More often than not, it is this sense of isolation that makes the Desert so arduous. What, for example, is the toughest thing that a minor-league baseball player must endure as he reaches his mid-twenties and that call-up to the big leagues still seems so far away? It is not the low salary, endless bus rides, fast-food diet, or back-breaking workouts orchestrated by his implacable coach. It is that cacophony of voices from well-meaning friends, and perhaps even his wife, endlessly reminding him that "if you were going to make it, you'd have made it by now" and that it is high time to "face facts" and "get on with your life." It is the agony of lying in bed night after night in some cheap motel wondering if maybe they are right: perhaps life is "passing him by" as he pursues a vain and even vainglorious dream. It is these inevitable and, yes, even necessary, dark nights of the soul that make the Desert so difficult, and this is why monks pray so fervently for the "discernment" that will lead them to the right decision.

One reason I find the scene between Hathaway's character and her father so poignant is that I had the exact same discussion many times with my own father and well-meaning friends when I put off graduating from college—where I ostensibly "had it made"—to become a carpet installer in order to study Zen for five years under a West Virginia hillbilly. What to my father was a blue-collar job, comparable to that of a secretary, I saw as an opportunity for self-development.

As with Hathaway's character and the fashion industry, I had no interest in installing carpet per se. Instead I saw it as an intrinsic aspect of my Zen training: an opportunity to overcome my fear of working with my hands; a way to stay in shape; a portable skill set that would allow me to travel as I sought teachers like Louis Mobley and other kindred spirits; a way to free my mind to pray and ponder life's mysteries as my body automatically installed carpet.

Like Hathaway's character, I started at the bottom as a humble installer's helper. Unlike her I was fired twice for slicing more fingers than carpet. Finally I found myself in Cleveland in the middle of winter, amidst a severe recession in the early 1970s. I was living in a drafty old ice-cream parlor that my Zen teacher called a "piano box," out of money, and recently fired yet again for being "too damn slow."

Meryl Streep's role as an impossibly demanding teacher was played in my case by carpet installing itself, but though I spent sleepless nights wondering whether to quit and "get on with my life" back in college, something held me back. Instead I picked up the Yellow Pages and called every carpet store within 50 miles, only to be rejected by every one. But after yet another dark night of the soul, I started calling them all over again. When I reached the *K*s, I got Mr. Kilgore, of Kilgore Carpets, on the line. Within seconds he interrupted.

"Hey," he growled. "Didn't I talk to you last week?"

"Yes, sir, you did," I replied.

"Didn't I tell you I didn't have anything?" he said even more irritably.

"Yes, you did, sir."

"Then why in hell's name are you bothering me again?"

"A lot of things can change in a week, sir."

For a few seconds there was silence. Then a voice softly said, "How soon can you get down here?"

Thanks to Mr. Kilgore's patience and my tenacity, I was gradually transformed into a carpet installer. And when it came time to move on in search of fresh challenges, Mr. Kilgore asked to see me. He was opening a new store and wanted me to manage it. Though I was moved by his offer, I declined. We shook hands and I turned to go, but then he said, "Wait a minute."

"Listen," he said gruffly, "I don't know where you're going or what you're going to do, but promise me one thing: if things don't work out, don't be too damn proud to come back here to us."

Like the little smile Anne Hathaway's character receives from Meryl Streep's at the end of *The Devil Wears Prada*, this was how Mr. Kilgore gave me his "passing grade." Like Hathaway's character, my tenacity had been rewarded, and like her I walked out that door a different person. I continued to lay carpet, but as a subcontractor in business for myself.

When I look back over my own business career, I owe more of my success to that goat rodeo of carpet installation than to anything else. Carpet installation taught me how to treat customers, sell myself, manage my boss, watch costs, supervise employees, establish credit, keep books, get out invoices, collect receivables, and how to buy a truck on December 31 in order to qualify for a tax credit from the Internal Revenue Service. By studying Zen I accidently mastered the Zen of business as a by-product of aiming past the target; but most importantly I learned, like the character played by Hathaway, to believe in myself, always give my best, and "never, ever quit."

Like Hathaway's character I went looking for the Kingdom and ended up with a Swiss Army knife of skills and character traits that paid off in thousands of ways I could never have anticipated. Carpet installation was one goat rodeo that took place in the Desert on my own transformational journey.

Finally, carpet installing was not something I did in order to study Zen. It was a way *to* study Zen. Zen teaches that we must "walk, not wobble" and that "your ordinary life is your spiritual life," and this is exactly what the Zen of Carpet Installation taught me. Every challenge we face is also an opportunity for transformation if we just learn to look at it in the right way.

○

IT WAS FIVE O'CLOCK on a Friday evening when I got a call from my goat-rodeo friend at Microsoft. He was about to distribute a hundred thousand CDs featuring Microsoft's latest technology at trade shows all over the world. He needed a third-party product built with Microsoft's technology to feature on the CDs, and he offered to use our product Visual Intercept to fill that hole. Besides all the free marketing, this implicit endorsement from Microsoft was huge, so I eagerly agreed. But then he said, "The product can't be bigger than three megs, I need it VeriSigned, and I need it today."

"But it's already five o'clock," I gasped.

"No problem," he blandly replied. "It's only two o'clock here, and I'll be working until midnight. Good luck." Then he hung up.

Our programmers promised to provide a working demo even though it meant stuffing a seven-megabyte product into a three-megabyte box. But the real problem was VeriSign. VeriSign is a company that provides the equivalent of a Good Housekeeping Seal of approval for software, and when my partner, Jay Hall, called the company he was told that the approval process took three weeks. Luckily, VeriSign was a West Coast company, and for the next several hours, Jay inched his way up the chain of command, only to be told at each step that the approval process took three weeks. Undaunted, he finally reached the president, and when Jay happened to mention that the ultimate customer was Microsoft, the president promised to turn things around in a couple of hours.

And somewhere just shy of three o'clock in the morning, we delivered the bits to Microsoft.

That was our first goat rodeo, and after a few more, we made our bones at Microsoft. We became the go-to guys whenever the folks at Microsoft were up against an apparently impossible deadline. Everyone in our company competed to be included in these heroic efforts, and the by-product was that our Microsoft alliance eventually made us millions.

5

MISSION

MY GOAL in the previous chapter was to introduce a transformational model of human motivation that defines the *what* of service and selflessness, and to show *why* this management philosophy is critical to the business success of the monastic tradition. Assuming that I accomplished these goals, what remains is to provide a detailed road map describing *how* we can apply service and selflessness to our secular organizations and even our personal lives with equally explosive results. The balance of this book is designed to do just that. The first step toward building a consciously transformational organization based on service and selflessness is making sure we have a high, overarching mission worthy of being served.

I WAS THE GUEST speaker recently at a three-day board and management retreat for the Winston-Salem, North Carolina–based Truliant Federal Credit Union. Rather than going straight to "the numbers," as I'd come to expect from similar gatherings, the entire first day was devoted to revisiting and reinforcing Truliant's lofty mission: "The Mission of Truliant Federal Credit Union is to enhance the quality of life of our members and become their preferred financial institution."

Truliant's CEO, Marc Schaefer, used his keynote to remind his team that people can accomplish just about any "what" if they believe in the "why" of their mission. He called this management philosophy the "Power of Why." He went on to tell Truliant's story from the beginning, vividly connecting the dots between the company's mission and its financial success.

According to Schaefer, for example, it was Truliant's mission that spared the company from the excesses of the financial bubble that crippled so many of the company's peers and drove others into bankruptcy. Truliant takes its mission of enhancing the quality of life of its members so seriously that, in the midst of the financial meltdown and while under great financial pressure, the company rejected a lucrative offer for its credit-card business for fear that Truliant's members would no longer get the kind of service they deserved and had come to expect. This is an example of selfless service that would make the monks of Mepkin proud, and in the long run, it was good for Truliant as well.

The balance of the day was spent giving each participant an opportunity to share their feelings about the company and its mission. Emotions ran so deep in some cases that I felt like I was listening to the monks of Mepkin Abbey speaking *ex cordia* ("from the heart") about their own lofty mission. Truliant was obviously more than a business. It was a way of life, offering every board member and employee the chance to make a profound difference in other people's lives.

Apparently I was not the only one who was impressed. During a break I encountered a new board member wandering around in the parking lot with a faraway look on his face. "Wow," he said, apparently to no one in particular. "I don't know what I was expecting, but it was not this. Everything I thought I knew about business is wrong."

Far from turning the company into a "touchy-feely" quasicharity, Truliant's mission has dramatically enhanced the bottom line of the business. In the midst of the most severe economic downturn since the Great Depression, Truliant averaged 9 percent annual deposit growth over the last four years, and it recently was named the fastest-growing credit union in the region it serves. When Truliant's members were asked if the company "has my best interest at heart," 95 percent strongly agreed or agreed. To put this remarkable number into perspective, in 2011, according to Forrester Research, Bank of America's customers were asked if "My financial provider does what is best for me, not just its own bottom line." Only 26 percent agreed. Wells Fargo managed only 31 percent.

In 2011 alone Truliant's employees proactively conducted 137,000 financial "checkups" for members, identified 197,000 "financial needs," and satisfied more than 100,000 of them—all with the single-minded goal of helping members "build a strong financial future." Almost as astounding as these figures is that a financial institution even has such a customer-centric program, let alone the metrics to measure its effectiveness. I ran my own business for seven years, and I never got a single call from any of my bankers offering a similar service.

But perhaps most impressive is Truliant's "delight index," based on customer responses to these four questions:

1. Overall, how satisfied are you with Truliant Federal Credit Union?
2. How strongly do you agree with the statement "Truliant has my best interest at heart"?
3. How likely is it that you would recommend Truliant to a friend, family member, or co-worker?
4. Do you feel like you are a part of Truliant?

Truliant's most recent score on this "delight index" was 76 percent. In chapter 2 we saw that very similar questions are used to measure employee engagement. Employees are paid for their loyalty, yet the level of loyalty from Truliant's paying members dwarfs that of most paid employees. Most corporate executives would give their right arm to have employees half as loyal as Truliant's customers.

Service and selflessness works, not just for Trappist monks but for secular organizations like Truliant as well. But when I asked, in light of their success, why more companies don't follow their lead, a board member summed it up. "It's sad, but most corporations just don't have the stomach for it, so they never bother to try."

A few days later, I was in Washington, DC, for my nephew's graduation from college. When I mentioned Truliant, my brother Mark interrupted. "Wow, you're working with Truliant? Everywhere I go somebody's gushing about those guys. Truliant's one helluva company."

◯

I DON'T REMEMBER much about third grade, but I'll never forget the first time the bookmobile showed up. I was instantly hooked on heroic tales from history, literature, and mythology, and my life might still be described as a quest for heroic undertakings and heroic people. One of my greatest heroes is Father Francis Kline, Mepkin's former abbot and a true Renaissance man. Dom Francis continually reminded the monks that "Your God is too small!" and his advice is equally applicable to our business, professional, and personal missions. In basketball we are urged to aim for the back of the rim, in golf to aim for the back of the cup, and in archery to aim past the target. But in business we aim for profit. Profit is not the goal of a business. It is merely a yardstick that measures how well we are accomplishing our mission. Truliant's ultimate goal is not profit. The ultimate goal is not even to become its customers' "preferred financial institution." Instead the company aims past both these targets in its quest to "enhance the quality of life" of its customers.

According to the company's chief marketing officer, Karen DeSalvo, Truliant "believes that if we focus on enhancing the lives of our members, becoming their preferred financial institution will simply 'fall out' as a result." In other words, becoming their customers' preferred financial institution and making a profit are merely the by-products and trailing indicators of Truliant's much bigger mission. The single biggest reason why so few businesses ever reach their full potential is because, unlike Truliant's, their mission is too small.

Every monastery begins with the highest possible mission: Serve God. This mission is clearly and unambiguously articulated, and anyone joining the monastery understands this coming in. To share in this mission is the reason why aspiring monks join and interlopers like me hang around by the thousands. This stands in sharp contrast to our business culture, in which even the CEOs are hard-pressed to rattle off their corporate mission statement—let alone live by it.

The most critical task for any organization is to continually ask, "What is the business of the business?" And everyone even remotely connected with the business must be involved in the answer. Only by continually asking this question and coming up with the biggest answers possible do we keep from defining the business too narrowly. It is this constant exercise that keeps us from defining the business as buggy whips when everyone is busy buying automobiles. In a world where the rate of change keeps accelerating, mission is now more important than ever.

For example, in the early days of the personal computer, companies such as Lotus, WordPerfect, and Netscape assumed that their mission was producing the best stand-alone spreadsheet, word-processing package, or Web browser. While linearly adding features as fast as they could, they failed to notice that Microsoft had nonlinearly figured out what users really wanted: the seamless integration of all these separate components. By questioning the assumptions underlying stand-alone software, Microsoft Office relegated an entire industry of stand-alone companies and their pioneering products to the scrap heap of history.

In today's ever-changing marketplace, most companies do not fail because they don't add features fast enough to their products. They fail because—like WordPerfect, Lotus, and Netscape or, more recently, Blockbuster, Borders, and even Microsoft itself—their product becomes a feature in a competitor's bigger and more robust offering. They fail because they are blindsided by a larger mission that emerges from a completely unanticipated direction. They fail because their god is too small.

In my consulting business, there is one objection I hear over and over: lofty mission statements are all "meaningless fluff." Most corporations are in niche markets with niche products, and high, overarching missions strike many as too soft, too abstract, too lofty, and too unfocused. Yet there is no mission more lofty, soft, and abstract than serving God by serving others, and monasteries manage to successfully infuse this lofty mission into a panoply of niche products and daily tasks with the kind of preternatural focus that produces almost supernatural results. The Marine Corps manages to infuse something as lofty and abstract as serving the country, the Corps, and your fellow marines into something as mundane as push-ups. Truliant is trouncing its peers by selflessly enhancing the quality of its members' lives, one human being at a time—often in utterly nonfinancial ways.

The reason why so many corporate mission statements seem vague and irrelevant and fail to inspire is not because they are too lofty or too abstract. It is because the executives tasked with infusing mission into execution lack the commitment and imagination it takes to make this happen. They are so busy "getting things done" that they fail to convey why the organization is doing all these things in the first place. As a result, whenever the long-term values of mission encounter the short-term exigencies of execution, expediency always wins. Defining mission and infusing it into decision making is not the province of a yearly management retreat. As Truliant's people demonstrate, it is a daily imperative that is the single most important priority every organization must have. And it depends just as much on the folks in the mail room as it does on the folks in the boardroom.

As I noted before, the secret to Mepkin Abbey's success is that the monks are not in the egg, mushroom, fertilizer, or forestry business. Like great archers, they aim past all these targets. They are in the business of serving God by serving one another and their neighbors. They are spiritual people who happen to run businesses; they are not profit-driven people who happen to have a sideline interest in service for PR purposes.

This radical reorientation of priorities is essential to monastic business success. It is dramatically counterintuitive and the most amazing example of outside-the-box thinking I've ever encountered. It is so revolutionary—and so frightening—that taking it to heart in our own businesses takes the strong stomach that the Truliant board member alluded to.

Charity, or what in its much larger sense the monks call *caritas*, means living from the heart. Living from the heart requires the change of heart that is the goal of the Hero's Journey. This transformational change of heart is what men join monasteries to attain and what the monastic life provides. Caritas is not something the monks practice part time for some future merit in the afterlife. It is who they are, and the driving force behind everything they do.

For the rest of us, as corporate citizens, charity is a wonderful thing, but we lack the "stomach" to put it at the heart of our businesses, despite the evidence of a 1,500-year monastic economic experiment and companies like Truliant to the contrary.

○

THE TRAPPIST MONASTERY OF Gethsemani in Kentucky was founded in the nineteenth century and traces its heritage back to the French Cistercian monastery of La Trappe. Convinced that their order had become too soft, the monks of La Trappe reformed the Cistercians by returning to the rigorous simplicity of their eleventh-century founders. These reforms were so successful that La Trappe became the inspiration for countless "daughter houses" or "foundations" like Gethsemani all over the world. The nickname "Trappist" is a tribute to La Trappe, though all Trappist monasteries technically belong to the Order of Cistercians of the Strict Observance (OCSO).

Gethsemani became world famous in the 1950s and 1960s when Thomas Merton, a writer and New York intellectual, entered Gethsemani to become a Trappist monk. Though he initially was barred from writing, the ban was eventually lifted, and his best-selling books (such as *The Seven Storey Mountain*) brought ancient monastic spirituality to a modern and increasingly secular world. It was Merton and his fascination with Zen that captured my imagination while I was still in college, and I owe my own fascination with the monastic way of life to him.

Mepkin Abbey in turn is a daughter house of Gethsemani, founded in 1949 by a small group of monks who voluntarily left their home in the rolling bluegrass hills of Kentucky for the swampy lowlands of South Carolina. Some of these pioneers, like Brother Joseph and Brother Robert, are still with us, and occasionally you will still see them communicating in the Trappist sign language that was used for centuries before the reforms of Vatican II in the early 1960s lifted the blanket prohibition on speaking aloud. These monks actually knew Thomas Merton before he was killed in a tragic accident while attending a conference with Buddhist monks in Bangkok, Thailand, in 1968.

Whenever they are willing and the remaining strictures on talking are relaxed, I ply these pioneers with questions about Merton and the "old days" at Gethsemani and bask in that faint hint of uncharacteristic pride that animates their stories about an even more heroic era, when men were still men and monks were still monks. But most moving are their descriptions of the tent city that even a monastery as large as Gethsemani had to erect to house a sudden influx of World War II veterans seeking, like Brother Edward, a meaningful antidote to the meaningless horrors of war.

It was Gethsemani that Mepkin's future abbot, Francis Kline, entered when he decided to become a Trappist monk in his early twenties. While entering a Trappist monastery is never a trivial decision, in Francis's case, it almost defies belief. Francis grew up in a prosperous family in Philadelphia. He studied music at the renowned Juilliard School, and by his late teens, he was a world-class prodigy on the organ. His Bach recitals from marquee venues were simulcast around the country, and he was sitting on a contract from a major recording label. Yet like his predecessor as abbot, Father Christian, and like Merton himself, Francis found the pull too strong. He boarded a bus for Kentucky and an utterly new life, a life that was anything but easy.

For starters he was barred from playing the organ. Even when this proscription was relaxed, he found himself playing fourth string behind three other monks—even though, as he laughingly told me one time, "I could blow them out of the water playing with one hand." Worse, at their first private meeting, his drill sergeant of a novice master said that he was utterly convinced that Francis didn't have what it took to be a Trappist monk, and that he was making it his business to prove it. It got so bad in the Desert that, like a latter-day Israelite, Francis thought things were looking better "back in Egypt." So one night Francis strode out the front gate. He walked six miles in a driving rainstorm before he laughingly thought, "Where the hell am I going?" and turned around and walked back.

But as difficult as these stories may sound, what struck me as I listened to them and others was the overwhelming love that Francis had for Gethsemani and his curmudgeon of a novice master. Like a newly minted marine fresh from boot camp or a devotee of AA's Twelve Step program, the fiery furnace of an authentically transformative experience had left Francis only with boundless gratitude.

When I first met Dom Francis in 1996, he was a tall, handsome man in his late forties, and his full head of hair, untarnished by gray, made him look ten years younger. Years before, he had gone off to Rome to become a priest and returned speaking Italian and several other languages as well. Fond of running, he was in great shape. He had a book to his credit and wrote and performed music on the splendid organ he had purchased for the monastery's new church. His love of art and architecture were reflected in the awards that the newly renovated church had received and in the tasteful way he was rebuilding much of the monastery.

Yet it was the charisma that arises only from authenticity that impressed me most about Francis. I'm not easily awestruck, but despite his kindness and affability, I always felt a bit tongue-tied in his presence, even in later years, when we were almost on familiar terms. *Holiness* is a word that is woefully out of style, and in any case not one that I would casually use. Yet it remains the only word I can come up with to capture that golden drop of something that distinguished Father Francis. As Brother Stephen, Mepkin's lovable prior and second in command, told me almost conspiratorially and with a trace of awe, "Francis is a mystic, you know."

Mission as Membrane

IN THE EARLY 1990S, Father Christian retired as abbot, and the Mepkin community sent word to Gethsemani that they wanted

Francis to take his place. He agreed on one condition: the community must be open to change. As he recounted to me once, "I told them I had no desire to supervise a dying monastery." The community agreed, and Francis set out to create a new mission for Mepkin while remaining true to the overall mission, or *charism,* of the Trappists.

The best way to describe his fresh approach is through the concept of a membrane. A membrane is not a lifeless wall. It is an organic structure that shares energy and nutrients with its environment while still filtering out harmful substances. While I never heard him say as much, Francis's mission was to replace the cloister wall that traditionally hermetically seals monks in with a living, breathing membrane—a membrane that freely interacts with the world yet still remains true to the essentials of the monastic tradition.

With the buy-in of the community, Francis started making changes. Much of the monastery was rebuilt; the land was restored to its pristine state, in keeping with Francis's keen environmental concerns; the library was vastly expanded; and a state-of-the-art conference center was built to strengthen Mepkin's ties with the local community and the larger world. Most importantly (for me at least), Mepkin created its monastic guest program, through which laymen (women can be retreatants but the monastic guest program is open only to men) can live and work alongside the monks for extended periods. But the real magic that surrounded Dom Francis's reading of the monastic mission is the most difficult to describe. Somehow Francis infused an invigorating spirit of excitement, change, and progress into Mepkin Abbey while remaining true to a tradition that relies on the changeless repetition of the monastic day to emphasize what is unchanging, eternal, and timeless.

This analogy to the membrane is equally applicable to our own personal missions and the missions of our organizations.

In the old days, a company could start out making buggy whips and five generations later still be making buggy whips. As recently as the 1960s and 1970s, most change was slow and incremental. Efficiency and execution rightly took precedence over mission. In my father's day and even into my own, most people retired from the same company they started with, lived in the same house throughout their adult lives, and held onto their old stoves and refrigerators for dear life. Change in a predominately static world is usually a bad thing, and, as in a monastery, walls were constructed around businesses to keep know-how and talent in while keeping business heresies and devil-worshipping corporate headhunters out.

The dawn of the Information Age over the last forty years has made this evolutionary model obsolete. The rate of change is increasing exponentially, and the strategic concerns of mission have overtaken the tactics of mere execution. Business today is replete with paradoxical terms—creative destruction, controlled chaos, "coopetition," disruptive technologies, jumping outside the system, fuzzy logic, breaking the frame, open systems, getting outside the box, and yes, even the Zen of business. All these terms point to a transformation in business itself—from the closed, static, and inorganic models that acted like the cloistering walls of a monastery to open, organic models that rely on membranes. Hell, we all used to work from something resembling a monk's cell called an "office." Now those spaces are rapidly being replaced with a membrane: the "virtual" office that floats freely in "the cloud" like a guardian angel that follows us wherever we go.

Today static, top-down missions that emerge from a bunch of cloistered executives at a management retreat are being replaced by bottom-up membranes that constantly share energy with the environment of the marketplace. A few years ago, even the term *bottom-up* meant listening to employees. Now, largely as a result of the Internet, companies increasingly rely on membranes that keep them constantly in dialogue with customers, vendors, the financial community, and every other aspect of a world that lies beyond the four walls of the business.

Louis R. Mobley said that managers get things done while executives decide on missions worth doing, and if this was true for IBM in 1956, it is a thousand times more true and important today. Effective leadership in the Information Age requires a value shift, from focusing on internal factors to focusing on the world at large, and this is just another way of describing what Father Francis's vision did for Mepkin. Like Father Francis, today's leaders must be generalists and Renaissance men rather than business specialists: After all, a butterfly flapping its wings over some savannah in Africa might just create the winds of change that bring a business to its knees.

To make matters more complicated still, applying membranes to mission requires reordering relationships with employees as well. In prior eras there was a demarcation between our personal and professional lives, and "professionalism" meant maintaining this hard-and-fast boundary. This is no longer true. Like monks living and working side by side, husbands and wives both work, and they take their personal lives to work and their work home with them. People no longer work for money and find meaning only in church. Now we all want meaningful work. The walls between our personal and professional lives have been replaced by membranes.

These trends are even reflected in the financial reports we use to manage our businesses. Financial reporting began with the balance sheet, which emerged when change was still relatively rare. A balance sheet is a static model, a yearly snapshot of the business. As the rate of change increased, a yearly balance sheet was no longer adequate, and quarterly profit-and-loss statements were invented. Eventually the quarterly P&L couldn't keep up, so the daily Cash Statement emerged as an ongoing way to more accurately keep tabs on the business.

Today, with the benefit of technology, the "inorganic" snapshots of the past have been replaced by "organic" movies that monitor the business constantly in real time. The transparency that these real-time reports produce is yet another example of how the dynamic and organic model of membranes is replacing the static model of walls separating the business from its environment.

Great business leaders like Steve Jobs don't succeed by knowing different things. They succeed by thinking in utterly different ways. If skills and knowledge once reigned supreme, it is now all about values and attitudes. Like some latter-day business Einstein "reinventing the universe," Steve Jobs created a mission for Apple that is based on a radically different worldview. Barely ten years ago, Apple was a bit player in the computer business, clutching at the crumbs that fell from Microsoft's table. Today Apple's market cap far exceeds Microsoft's, and companies like Nokia—which narrowly construed cell phones as nothing but mobile telephones—are gasping for air as they pay the price for worshipping a god that was far too small. And according to Jobs, at a commencement speech he gave at Stanford, it all started when he decided to aim past the target by eclectically studying things like calligraphy in college for nothing more than self-development.

Personal Growth in Real Time

SOME PEOPLE HAVE GREATNESS thrust upon them; in my case it was entrepreneurship. Once I asked my old Zen master what was the most important thing he did on his own spiritual path. "It wasn't what I did," he replied. "It was what I didn't do." Then he walked away, leaving me mystified.

In 1985 I turned my back on a fast-track career in cable television and joined a software start-up in Research Triangle Park, North Carolina, as vice president of sales and marketing. As usual this was not part of any great strategic plan for my career. Instead it was just an aiming-past-the-target decision to learn an industry that was rapidly changing the world, and an opportunity to see what I could learn from living in the South. Several years later it became obvious that the company was failing. In 1987 I left and began doing some consulting for companies back in the cable television business.

A few months later, I was invited to speak to several groups of North Carolina State students through the University Scholars Program, a program designed to intellectually and culturally broaden the student body. I came up with a talk called "Five Years with a Zen Master," based on my adventures and misadventures studying Zen under a West Virginia hillbilly. The students seemed to enjoy it, and four of them approached me after one of the lectures and asked me to coach them on Zen in particular and spirituality generally. I agreed to meet with them every Thursday evening, and they formed a student club they called the Self Knowledge Symposium (SKS) in order to get a room on campus in which to meet.

Several weeks later, I got a telephone call from an old friend from the television business.

"Listen, Augie," he said, "I was just named CEO of United Press International, and I got $150 million to take it out of bankruptcy and turn it around."

He went on to say that he was "putting the band back together" by hiring a bunch of our mutual friends, and that he wanted me to be his executive vice president and second in command. The money was fabulous and the fun factor more than enticing, but there was one hitch: I would have to move from Raleigh, North Carolina, to Washington, DC. After a few moments, I regretfully informed him that I was unable to move.

"Why?" he asked.

I told him that I had just agreed to chair a weekly meeting for some college students.

"Are you kidding?" he said, "You're turning down a dream job to work for free for a couple of college kids? Jesus, why don't you just do whatever it is you do up here? We got lots of colleges in DC."

"I got a better idea, Joe," I replied. "Move UPI to Raleigh."

"No way," he laughed, "my wife would never go for that!"

"Aw, c'mon Joe, there are plenty of women in Raleigh."

Though we both had a hearty laugh, a few moments later the call was over, and it gradually settled in that I had indeed turned down a dream job for a couple of college kids I barely knew. Over the next week or so I agonized over my decision, longing to pick up the phone. The worst part was that I had no one to turn to for advice because I knew exactly what everyone I knew would say.

But despite my agony, I just couldn't go back on my word. Everything I'd learned and everything I'd *become* since college told me that I had to seek *first* the kingdom of heaven, and that meant keeping my promise to those kids, no matter what the consequences might be.

Over the next several years, the seed that was planted at NC State grew, and the SKS spread to the University of North Carolina and Duke University. Eventually a group of adults began meeting at my home every Friday night as well. While I couldn't have said so at the time, the theme of all this work was transformation. These meetings became the equivalent of AA meetings for people who didn't drink but were still longing to make fundamental changes in their lives. Unlike discussion groups, meditation groups, or prayer groups, our meetings quickly evolved into creating concrete action plans for transforming our lives while using the inspiration and peer pressure of community to help keep us on track.

For the first few years, I was able to earn a living through consulting, but eventually my teaching responsibilities meant that flying all over the country was no longer an option. Besides, as the word spread that I wouldn't move, my reputation suffered. One time, after turning down a job in Colorado, I called the executive who recommended me in order to thank him and to explain my decision. He quickly interrupted me.

"Don't worry, Augie," he said. "I covered my butt. I told him that you're great at what you do, but you're some kind of religious nut."

So as our little community grew, travel became too onerous, and the phone stopped ringing, I decided to become an entrepreneur.

Obviously, neither money nor any overt desire to become an entrepreneur led to my decision. Instead, I saw building a company as a demonstration project, a way to put all the principles that I espoused into practice. I saw it as a way to create goat-rodeo opportunities for personal growth in real time under the pressure of real-life challenges. I saw entrepreneurship as an acid test of my principles and of everything I had learned from people like my Zen teacher, from Louis R. Mobley, and from carpet installation. I wanted to know whether a company built on the principles of service and selflessness could really work. And, perhaps most importantly, I wanted to show our nascent community what could be accomplished if a group of high-minded individuals were willing to make the kind of ironclad commitments to each other that every authentic community, like Mepkin Abbey, must be built upon.

In the very beginning, there were just six of us, including my brother Tom. We didn't have a business plan beyond what one of my partners described as, "We're smart guys—we'll figure out something to do." We may have been vague on what we were going to do, but we were crystal clear about who we wanted to be. As Citizen Kane did when he bought his first newspaper, we came up with a statement of principles that we intended to live by.

Our first principle was that we wanted to create a spiritual company. This didn't mean that we expected everyone to buy into a particular religion or set of beliefs. It meant that personal growth, honesty, integrity, and selflessly putting people first were more important than making money. It also meant that our company would be "spiritually friendly"; no one need feel embarrassed or ashamed about talking philosophy at the watercooler or taking time off to go on a retreat. Creating a spiritually friendly environment may seem trivial, but over the years dozens of visitors expressed surprise at the kinds of books I had on my bookshelf, which, suffice it to say, didn't exactly match the literary tastes they expected in a CEO.

Our second principle was high expectations. Starting a business based on spiritual values didn't mean setting low bars and rationalizing away failure as just one of the inevitable costs of trying to do spiritual business in a profane world. Instead, if we were truly in business for a higher purpose, our goals should be higher than the goals of those who were simply in it for the money. For example, we decided to begin work each morning at seven-thirty in order to get a jump start on those heathens better known as the competition. We maintained that start time for the next seven years.

Our third principle was compassion. This didn't mean that we would never fire anyone. It meant that we would do everything we could to help everyone get over the bar—without lowering the bar. While more would be expected of some than of others, all would be expected to carry his or her own weight.

Our fourth principle was a corollary of the third. We wanted our company to be a community; the whole would be greater than the sum of its parts. A community capable of extending compassion to individuals must also be composed of people willing to sacrifice for the good of the community. Carrying one's own weight, for example, is one way for an individual to show compassion for the community.

Our fifth principle was keeping promises through a management system that formalized accountability. We decided to wage a relentless war against the ambiguity, equivalence, and outright double-talk that we all use to get off the hook. We wanted a goal-setting culture that eschewed "I'll try" in favor of "I'll do."

Keeping promises was often inconvenient. For example, we paid every one of our vendors on time, even when it was very tempting to "stretch" our payables. We did this even when, especially in the early years, it meant that my partners or I didn't get a paycheck. We always paid our vendors on time simply because this is what we had promised to do.

Our sixth principle was open communication. Professionally this meant having all those "awkward" business conversations that usually end up under the rug. To keep the lines of communication open, we also had to give everyone permission to make mistakes. On the personal level, this meant that our employees would always find a sympathetic ear when issues outside the business were impinging on their productivity or merely weighing on their minds.

Our seventh principle was honesty—no hidden agendas and trumped-up business cases designed to mask selfish motivations. We were perfectly sympathetic to someone who needed or wanted more money, a bigger office, or a window office. What was intolerable was sitting through a three-hour presentation ostensibly designed to make the sales force more efficient but really designed to slyly get the presenter a bigger share of the pie. Put another way, our seventh principle just meant no B.S.!

We called our eighth principle "Anybody can fight." Bickering and political infighting are easy. Compromise and conflict resolution are hard. From the very beginning, we made it clear that if any two individuals or departments couldn't resolve their differences on their own, both parties would suffer regardless of the eventual outcome.

Our final principle was to embrace a "back against the wall" mentality. Peak performance is usually a delicate balance between inspiration and desperation, and from the very beginning, like Cortés burning his ships, we wanted to build a sense of urgency into our company. As a result, though one of my partners and I were relatively well off, we invested only enough capital for one month's office rent and phones. This came to only a couple of thousand dollars, and we decided that if we ever couldn't bring in enough money to pay the next month's expenses, we would close the company rather than prop it up with continual cash infusions.

A Zen master once said, "Seek the Truth like your hair is on fire." Believe me, knowing that bills are coming due and that no more seed capital is forthcoming is guaranteed to set your entrepreneurial hair ablaze. For the first six months, we survived on pure hustle. At one point I spent weekends canvassing for a burglar alarm company for $7.00 an hour just to pay the rent.

◯

ONE OF THE BEST things I ever did was turn down that job at UPI. The reorganized UPI soon went bankrupt, and the company we started on a few grand was eventually acquired by an Israeli company that was in turn acquired by software giant BMC. With the benefit of hindsight, I now see the whole episode surrounding UPI as just one of the Great Trials or temptations that stud the Hero's Journey. A wise old veteran of the entrepreneurial wars once prophesized that every entrepreneur must be willing to die a thousand deaths on his way to success, and as we shall see in later chapters, over the years my partners and I were tested time and again. Each time his prophecy was borne out. These temptations, like taking the job at UPI, always looked like the "smart play" or "safe bet" but would have meant compromising our mission. Next to the Hero's Journey itself, the toughest thing I've ever endured was building a company entirely on internally generated cash. The process was often downright excruciating, and we were often lost in the Desert, critically short of cash rather than water.

As my Zen master said, in the end it isn't what we do but what we don't do that makes all the difference. It took me thirty years to decipher his enigmatic Zen koan, but I think I now know what he "didn't do" that made all the difference to his life. He never sold out.

6

SELFLESSNESS AND COMMUNITY

ON MY FIRST VISIT to Mepkin Abbey, I found myself in the lunch line behind a frail monk clearly well into his eighties. While he slowly and painfully stooped for one of the trays stacked knee-high beneath the counter, I was busily trying to stifle my impatience. But when he finally retrieved it, he didn't move forward. Instead, to my surprise, he suddenly turned and presented me with his hard-earned tray with a look of childlike delight.

Over the next several days, I witnessed so many similar acts of kindness that I began to find it contagious. It wasn't the kindness per se that inspired me, but the simple, natural, and spontaneous way this kindness permeated the monastery. Before I knew it, I was visiting more often, staying longer, volunteering for extra work, and giving away trays as fast as I could. The monks' commitment to community was so contagious that I couldn't help myself. The atmosphere was so transformative that I was being transformed without any conscious effort on my part.

Father Guerric is an urbane and sophisticated former parish priest who took me under his wing during my first visits to Mepkin.

One day he told me a story that helped me understand where this atmosphere of monastic kindness all around me came from.

When Guerric first arrived at the monastery, he wanted to make high-end vinegars and other condiments for Mepkin to sell. But when he presented his idea to the abbot at one of their initial meetings, Father Francis said, "That's a great idea. But what we really need is an infirmarian."

"So off to school I went, and now I change bedpans," Guerric said with a gentle smile. "I came here to serve God by serving others, not to play Farmer John. I should've walked in there and asked Francis how I could help the community. Even after all this time, I'm still ashamed of myself."

$\bigcirc$

SELFLESSLY SERVING THE COMMUNITY is critical to Mepkin Abbey's business success. All too often what cripples a business is too many people anxiously worrying about their own success and keeping a watchful eye on anyone who might threaten their position. This internal friction is nonexistent at Mepkin, which means that everyone is focused exclusively on serving customers and stakeholders. This doesn't mean that monks are soulless automatons without individual needs that must be accommodated. It just means that Mepkin's culture continually demonstrates that the shortest route to achieving these individual goals is by serving the overall community and its mission. A recent article in the *Wall Street Journal* described this phenomenon well: "The shortest distance between two points is taking the long way around." The more we put others first, the more quickly we reach our personal goals. Apparently it worked for Father Guerric. After his stint as infirmarian and at the community's request, he now manages the gift shop, stocking it with gourmet products straight from the garden he was finally able to plant.

As a sales executive for many years, I spent most of my time trying to unravel the riddle of human motivation. I tried all the traditional levers—recognition, rewards, and quotas—with pedestrian results until I finally stumbled on the answer: maximum performance emerges from the peer pressure of a community working toward a common mission.

It was only when I realized that, like a marine, we will do things for our buddies and the Corps that we would never do for ourselves that we got the results we were looking for. I stopped managing individuals and started managing culture. I concentrated on building community, and when I did, revenue took care of itself. Just like at Mepkin Abbey.

Part of what makes putting community first so difficult is that the very idea is deeply counterintuitive. For most of us, it may seem like the purpose of community is to serve the individual. But monastic business success hinges on the counterintuitive notion that the purpose of the individual is actually to serve the community. In chapter 3, I argued that it only *seems* like we all want an easy life of self-indulgence. But a bit of monklike contemplation soon discerns the counterintuitive truth: we are actually happiest and most satisfied when we are sacrificing for something bigger than ourselves. And as communal creatures, we discover that one of those things worth sacrificing for is community.

It may seem, for example, like the end user and primary beneficiary of the work of Habitat for Humanity is the needy person who gets a house. But the other, very real, beneficiaries are all the people being transformed, one nail at a time, by the communal experience of building a house for a worthy mission. This is a benefit that merely writing a check can never bestow. It was because these communal benefits were so firmly in place at Mepkin Abbey that it felt like I was being transformed with so little effort on my part.

As someone who has spent much of my life both professionally and personally trying to build sustainable communities, what is particularly distressing to me is that most of the folks who undermine communities are good people who mean well. It is just that the notion that communities exist exclusively to serve individuals seems so intuitive, obvious, and commonsensical that we take advantage of our communities without realizing it.

Again, in many ways this is understandable. Psychologists have actually coined the term *identifiable individual* to explain why we will incur far greater costs to save one identifiable person than we will to save many more anonymous people, people psychologists refer to as *statistical lives*. While no expense is spared saving an identifiable coalminer trapped in a mine, we are often reluctant to spend far less on mine safety to protect people we will never see on television or encounter personally.

All too often in corporate or even nonprofit organizations, employees are the identifiable individuals, while customers are treated like an amorphous cloud of disembodied statistical lives. In 1984 I was vice president of marketing for a large cable television operator, and I visited one of our systems in New Jersey. During a meeting I questioned the highly punitive way in which late-paying customers were treated: tardy customers were quickly disconnected and forced to come groveling to the office in person to have their service reinstated. My concern was greeted by a fusillade of complaints about the "added work" that delinquent customers created for the staff. I listened silently until the furor had subsided and then quietly said, "I think I understand. If we just get rid of all these darn customers, the business will run far more smoothly." To their credit, my colleagues decided to relax their policy considerably.

Father Francis once told me that monasticism is at heart counterintuitive, or, more accurately, countercultural. Living selflessly is not natural, and its benefits are often not obvious. If they were, everyone would be selfless. As with my cable television colleagues in the example above, it takes some contemplation to realize that selfishness only seems to hold the secret to success. And even when we realize that it is actually selflessness that we really want, it takes discipline to turn this realization into second-nature instinct.

The same holds true for community. Paradoxically, we need communities to teach us the value of community, and this is a large chunk of what the Rule of St. Benedict, Marine boot camp, and AA's Twelve Step program are designed to do. And like the novice we met in a previous chapter, still pushing ninety-year-old monks aside to get that last dish of ice cream, we find that becoming a community-oriented person requires a lot of contemplation and just plain work. It is not easy to overcome our bias for benefiting individually at the expense of the overall community and its long-term mission.

The answer to the problem of the community versus the individual lies in holding the interests of the community and the interests of particular individuals or classes of individuals in balance. Despite their monastic mission to serve others, not every individual who wants to join the Mepkin community is accepted. Before entering, every applicant is screened by a psychologist. Most of these aspirants also have already spent time living among the monks as "observers" so that they and the community can discern whether there is a fit. It is rare, but occasionally a novice who has passed these preliminary screens may be asked to leave because the interests of the community outweigh the interests of an individual monk.

It is up to the abbot, with the input of his brothers, to hold the interests of the community and particular individuals in balance. But it is important to remember that community service for the monks doesn't just mean serving each other as unique individuals, or even their customers and neighbors. It also means sacrificing for abstract concepts such as "Mepkin Abbey," "monasticism," "the community," "the Cistercian tradition," "the Church," "the Life," and for all those people yet to be born who may one day benefit from the long-term survival of a place like Mepkin. When marines sacrifice purely for the good of the "country and the Corps," they are sacrificing for a sense of community that is far bigger than the sum of the individuals that make up the community as they know it.

Similarly, corporations do not exist only to provide their employees with jobs. The interests of employees must be held in balance with the often-anonymous interests of customers, stockholders, vendors, and stakeholders as well. At times all the individuals that make up these constituencies must be able to put aside their individual goals in the interest of the overall mission. If they do not, the corporation has little hope of being able to continue being of service to any individuals over the long term.

None of this is meant to imply that corporate loyalty is not also earned. As we saw in chapter 5, Marc Schaefer and his team at Truliant Federal Credit Union have earned the loyalty of their employees and customers by consistently staying true to their lofty mission of selfless service.

AS I MENTIONED PREVIOUSLY, for the first six months after starting our business, Raleigh Group International (RGI), all we did was scramble. We took little more than odd jobs, sometimes at minimum wage, just to keep the doors open—which we barely did. Our first break came when Kenny Felder offered us the opportunity to become a reseller of his own company's product, SourceSafe.

I met Kenny when he was still a college student at the University of North Carolina. A brilliant physics student and an atheist, Kenny welcomed the opportunity to be part of a group that addressed philosophical and spiritual subjects without insisting that he abandon his skepticism. Borrowing from my old Zen teacher, the only things I insisted that students accept without question were:

1. We can all be a little less stupid than we are today.
2. Self-knowledge is the most valuable knowledge of all.

After graduating, Kenny and his wife, Joyce, joined the adult group that met at my home every Friday night, which kept us in close contact. After working as a programmer for a year or so, he and two of his friends started One Tree Software in Kenny's living room to build SourceSafe. (SourceSafe is a version-control package, a software developer's tool that allows teams of programmers to work together on the same source code without overwriting each other.)

I admit that I was skeptical when he and his partners first set up shop, but I soon became a believer. Revenue at One Tree was increasing every month despite the fact that, as programmers, Kenny and his partners had no experience in sales and marketing. So even though we in turn knew nothing about developers' tools, we started reselling SourceSafe.

SourceSafe was a shrink-wrapped product retailing for only $300. Even though One Tree could offer us nothing in the way of marketing support, we managed to cold-call our way to $8,000 in sales our first month. We were thrilled, even though we had to send 60 percent of the take back to One Tree. At last we had something to sink our teeth into. The next month it was $14,000, and the next, $19,000. We were still working without pay, but it seemed like our community project was finally on its way.

Meanwhile the group of adults meeting in my living room was growing as well. Eventually we decided to throw $5.00 each into a hat every Friday to offset any expenses we might incur as a community. I asked for a volunteer to act as treasurer, and after the meeting Kenny stepped forward, on one condition.

"What's that?" I asked.

"If someone forgets their five bucks, I don't want to turn them away. I'll run a tab, and if someone leaves us in the lurch, I'll make it up out of my own pocket."

"That's very generous of you," I said, "but you can't be our treasurer."

"I don't get it," Kenny countered. "This is supposed to be a community; a brotherhood built on compassion. This isn't a movie theater."

"You're right," I said. "We're not a movie theater. We're better than a movie theater. Why would we treat a theater with more respect than we treat our community? Compassion starts by showing compassion to you as a symbol of our community. It's our job to make your job as easy as possible. And if we don't start building the right habits around the little things, we won't be around long enough to worry about the big things. If someone genuinely can't afford the five bucks, that's one thing, but just taking advantage of the community and calling it compassion is another."

Lou Mobley once told me that his goal at the IBM Executive School was to facilitate aha! moments that produce a "Wow, I never thought of it that way before!" reaction. This was what I got from Kenny. He accepted the job as treasurer, and once we made our policy clear, the issue never came up again.

This story is not meant to illustrate how much better or smarter I am than Kenny. On the contrary, Kenny is far smarter and a far better person than I and remains to this day one of my closest friends. Instead I tell this story to illustrate just how deeply ingrained, even in the best people, is the bias that communities only exist to serve individuals. Good people with good intentions are not enough. Becoming a community-oriented person requires its own transformation of being. It requires a different outlook, worldview, and habit of mind. It means working on becoming a good follower just as hard as you do at becoming a good leader.

○

LIKE FATHER GUERRIC in the throes of his own formation, struggling to put the interests of the community first, the members of our community began offering as much compassion to the community as they did to individuals only with great difficulty, amidst continual reminders. And meanwhile, the toughest part of my job as leader was facilitating that transformation in attitude and outlook while not coming across as insensitive to individuals.

About a year after we started RGI, a young woman from our Friday meetings joined as a sales rep. One day she came to my office and said that her father was dying and she needed a leave of absence. We granted her request, but after several months her father stabilized, and she returned to work. Six months later her father relapsed, and she requested another leave. I told her that I was deeply sympathetic, but that if she left again, I would have to fill her job. Understandably, she was deeply upset.

Several hours later one of my partners told me that he and the other sales reps thought I was being heartless and unfair.

"This is a community," he said. "We're supposed to take care of each other."

I explained that we did not have enough cash to both stay in business and have one of our four sales reps go on leave again.

"But I do have an idea," I said. "If you and the other reps just split up Janet's sales target and add it to your own, we can pull it off."

His eyes got as big as saucers.

I continued, "You are all assuming that it is the community's job to replace 25 percent of our revenue without replacing Janet. You guys want to extend compassion without the burden of paying for it."

He thought for a moment and then suddenly said, "I got it. No more unfunded mandates."

He returned and spread the word. We all pulled together, and somehow we managed to keep the company going and bring Janet back after her father eventually did pass away.

It was only little by little and through countless mutual reminders that our company was gradually transformed from a collection of well-intentioned individuals into an authentic community. And paradoxically, the stronger the community became, the easier it was to offer kindnesses to individuals, like unasked-for raises or surprise bonuses. The shortest distance between two points is the long way around.

The Danish philosopher Søren Kierkegaard used vivid biblical and mythological examples to argue that what makes living an ethical life so difficult is the countless ways in which the interests of individuals conflict with the interests of the community. The monks of Mepkin Abbey transcend this conflict by so selflessly serving their community that the community in turn can support monks like Father Guerric, living out his dream.

In my own case, trying to be fair both to individuals and the community was the toughest and most painful part of my job. It meant many a dark night of the soul as I agonized over decisions and then kicked myself when I was wrong. But the agony was worth it. After our initial success selling SourceSafe, we began selling other developers' tools from other companies. And over time a peculiar phenomenon began to take place. About three months after picking up a new product line, we would get a phone call from the president of the company.

"Listen," he would say, "your sales force is outselling our own by a wide margin. Would you mind sending us a copy of your pitch?"

This happened so often that it became a bit of a joke; after taking on a new product, we made small wagers on how soon we would get the call. In every case we happily shared our pitch. We would have shared our pitch from our commitment to service and selflessness anyway, but in these cases it was far easier. We well knew that there was nothing magical about our pitch. It wasn't what our reps said, but how they said it. It was the passion behind our selling that made all the difference.

Our numbers were better because we successfully resisted the temptation to manage individuals. Instead we focused on building a culture, a culture that only emerges from the peer pressure of a communal team working toward a common mission. And when we did, revenue took care of itself. Just like at Mepkin Abbey.

No one believes in the science of business more than I do. Our commitment to service and selflessness didn't mean avoiding the mind-numbing task of poring over reams of market research and financial reports looking for the tiniest comparative advantage. In fact, my own commitment to service and selflessness meant that I had a moral obligation to leave no stone unturned or technique untried. I cold-called every vice president of marketing in our industry, for example, looking for the tips that all but one graciously provided—tips that saved us an untold amount of time and money. But while I recommend this exercise in humility to every executive I meet, business science is not nearly enough. As the monks like to say, it is not just the prayer you say that matters. It is how passionately you pray. And just as at Mepkin, it is an authentic community, praying in unison, that prays most passionately of all.

○

I WAS ALWAYS A little intimidated by Brother Laurence. He had a long face, sad eyes, and a stately bearing and beard, and I sometimes wondered, if like the last surviving member of that order of warrior monks, the Knights Templar, his cross-emblazoned breastplate might still be lurking under his hooded habit. Even for a silent Trappist monk, Brother Laurence kept quietly to himself. Old-school to his fingertips, he apparently lived only for prayer and, especially, work. He worked ceaselessly, often spending his days astride Mepkin's bright yellow backhoe, heedlessly wheeling his caparisoned charger into battle against the giant oak logs slated for the wood-burning boiler that heats the church. These massive logs are the unfortunate casualties of the gale-force storms that periodically sweep in from the sea and envelop the monastery. After sawing up a fallen oak for firewood with his heavy, swordlike chain saw, Brother Laurence always carefully removed a sapling from the surrounding forest and marshaled his green recruit into service as a replacement.

Even though the other monks obviously felt a deep affection for Brother Laurence, I found him stern and forbidding—so much so that over the years, I had only one conversation with him, and that was decidedly brief.

Christmas Eve at Mepkin is the longest day of the year. Up at three in the morning, the monks maintain their unvarying routine throughout the day. Rather than retiring at eight in the evening as usual, however, they attend Christmas Eve Mass instead, ending at ten. After Mass the abbot hosts a Christmas party in the refectory, attended by monks and guests. Apple cider and various Christmas treats are served, and for an hour or two, everyone exchanges a large dose of Christmas cheer.

At one such party, I noticed Brother Laurence standing off by himself, observing the proceedings without joining in. I sidled over to him and wished him a merry Christmas. He responded in kind, but then lapsed into such a profound silence that even for a monastery built on silence, it became awkward. Suddenly he said, through a tight smile, "I don't like people much. They make me uncomfortable." And with that he excused himself and headed off for bed.

I don't think his remark was specifically aimed at me, but it sure felt that way. I decided that Brother Laurence was not only a knight but a knight errant, intent on pursuing the Holy Grail in a purely solitary fashion. But I couldn't have been more wrong about gallant Laurence.

Four times a year, Abbot Francis hosted a "chicken party." All hands would converge on one of the monastery's four chicken houses, and 10,000 of the old hens would be noisily extracted from their cages, loaded into trailer trucks, and shipped off for chicken soup. We worked in two-man teams, and as we were finishing up, I noticed Brother Laurence carefully setting aside a couple hundred cackling chickens. I asked Father Christian about it.

"Laurence has an amazing relationship with many of the poor African American families around here," he said. "Later today he'll load them into a truck and deliver fresh chicken to hungry people. Anything he can think of, he does for those people, and they love him for it."

I was stunned. I'd pegged Brother Laurence for a misanthropic loner, only to find that community service was everything to him. Our Lady of Mepkin is practically walled in by African American Baptist churches, but she has a wonderful relationship with her neighbors. I like to think that a lot of the credit belongs to the intrepid efforts of Brother Laurence. In Brother Laurence we find an individual whose definition of community and community service was so elastic that it extended far beyond the cloistered walls of Mepkin Abbey or even the monastery's business customers—encompassing "community" in its best and truest sense.

7

EXCELLENCE FOR THE SAKE OF EXCELLENCE

I hear and I forget.
I see and I remember.
I do and I understand.
—*Confucius*

BROTHER JOSEPH is Mepkin's version of St. Francis of Assisi. After meals you will unfailingly find him rummaging through the kitchen, collecting bread crusts and empty peanut butter jars for all the squirrels, deer, birds, opossums, and raccoons that converge on the magnificent oak tree that lives on the bluff overlooking the Cooper River, just outside his cloister door. Brother Joseph and his variegated congregation seem to have already anticipated that prophetic time, heralded by Isaiah, when swords will be beaten into plowshares and the lion will peacefully lie down with the lamb.

Joseph's ministry to the animal kingdom takes him far beyond the lively chapel provided by the oak's moss-strewn canopy—a revelation that proved as embarrassing for me as it was amusing for the monks. One day I was taking a meditative walk toward the Luce Gardens at dusk when I saw six sets of glowing eyes watching me from the woods. Squinting into the shadows, I was just vaguely making out their shapes when they suddenly burst, yelping, from the woods. At first I held my ground, but I quickly lost my nerve and made a hasty and rather undignified retreat back to the monastery—only to find that my wolflike pursuers were only a covey of motherless fox cubs that had mistaken me for Brother Joseph bringing their dinner.

Brother Joseph's gentle compassion doesn't just extend to his winged and four-legged friends. I have the terrible habit of letting my car's battery go dead from disuse when I visit Mepkin for extended periods. Whenever I do, Brother Joseph always gets out his charger and cheerfully rejuvenates my battery without even a hint of the impatience that I more than deserve for my serial sins of omission.

When he isn't attending to the needs of animals or other people, Brother Joseph is one of Mepkin's hardest workers. One day a truck arrived, its trailer stacked high with 50-pound bags of the limestone that Joseph mixed into the chicken feed for its calcium. Most of the community was assigned to help unload the truck, but it was Joseph who leaped onto the flatbed like a cat. He then hefted and handed down each bag as the rest of us took turns shouldering them onto a stack. Not a bad workout for a man of seventy or so whose wiry frame probably goes all of 140 pounds.

In all the years I've known him, I've only seen Joseph riled up once. This time my tires as well as my battery had run down, and Joseph had fired up the monastery's air compressor in order to breathe fresh life into my moribund tires. I fully intended to administer this resuscitation myself, but before I could move, Joseph was already squatting at a tire. I was struck yet again to see Joseph taking the lead and doing even the most trivial task with such enthusiasm, so I ventured to ask him about it.

"I've been a monk for over fifty years," he practically shouted, taking me off guard, "and I still don't like getting up at three o'clock in the morning! I was called to this life. Show me a monk without a vocation, and I'll show you an idiot or a madman. But everyone is called to something bigger than themselves. Those who say they're not just never learned to listen. This life taught me to love, and now it's easy to give my best even if I still don't like getting out of bed."

The Power of Sacrifice

WHEN WE WERE GROWING up, my seven younger siblings and I would walk every morning to the white-brick Catholic school perched on a hill just across a valley from our front stoop. In contrast to their forbidding reputation, our Franciscan nuns with their Irish brogues were almost without exception wonderful women who only reinforced the stereotype that God gifts the Irish with a ready wit and wicked sense of humor. Whenever I complained, the sisters always told me (though often only half seriously) to stop whining and "offer it up" to God instead. Though this admonishment usually had the desired effect, I could never understand their advice. Did it somehow please an all-loving God to see me suffer?

But I now think I have a better handle on what the sainted sisters were trying to teach me. The suffering that accompanies sacrifice has a unique quality. Discomfort of all kinds brings us "back to ourselves." It forces us to consciously consider what we are doing and why we are doing it. Sacrifice takes us out of our mindless immersion in the moment and invites us to contemplate the "big picture."

The right kinds of sacrifices, like a figurative stone intentionally placed in a shoe or a string tied to a finger, serve as reminders of what we want our lives to be about. In this sense the sacrificial suffering that the Hero's Journey requires is an antidote to the human tendency to be unconsciously swept along by the trivial exigencies of daily life until, like Rip Van Winkle, we sleep our lives away mired in one thing after another. The philosopher Nietzsche sarcastically quipped, "Blessed are the sleepy ones, for they shall soon drop off," and it is not an accident that religious traditions from all over the world describe spirituality as a process of awakening. Often it is only discomfort that can jar us out of our semisomnolent state and make us conscious and self-aware, or what the monks would call *mindful*.

The monastic vows of poverty, chastity, and obedience are often derided as atavistic relics from a time when an implacable, sadistic, and world-hating Christian god apparently relished the sight of human flesh being "mortified." But since these ascetic practices are common to many of the world's great religious traditions, there must be something else going on. Asceticism properly practiced is not a form of masochism for the practitioner's "sins." It is a way of intentionally building in a source of friction in order to stay awake to the effort that living a heroic life requires. In this sense attending AA meetings is an ascetic practice. The sacrifice required to attend 90 meetings in the first 90 days, as AA encourages, repeatedly reminds the recovering alcoholic of his commitment to sobriety while firmly wedging a figurative Popsicle stick into the habitual gears of automatic living that often lead right back to the bottle. Ritually making 10 cold calls a day can serve the same purpose in business. Cold-calling for clients can be nothing but an unpleasant chore, or it can be offered up as an exercise in overcoming the fear of rejection and failure that dogs us at every turn on the Hero's Journey. Again, it all depends on whether we remember to aim past the target with our aspirations.

The net effect is that the more we sacrifice for a goal or mission, the more passionate we become about that goal or mission. Imagine a college freshman intent on becoming a doctor someday. His course load is heavy with challenging courses, so, monklike, he ascetically renounces the nonstop partying that pervades his dorm. Every time he resists the temptation to join a party, he is painfully reminded of his goal. And the fruit of this sacrifice is that he redoubles his dedication to his studies. Why? Because he realizes that if he does not, he may very well end up with the worst of both worlds: no parties and no admission to med school. In other words, the more he sacrifices, the more serious he becomes about what he is sacrificing for.

We usually think that we sacrifice only for things that we care about. But, counterintuitively, we can learn to care about things by sacrificing for them. Sacrifice is an investment of time and energy added to the opportunity cost of all the other things we could be doing with that same time and energy. And we are all hardwired to protect such a precious investment. The more we sacrifice, the more we care; the more we care, the more passionately motivated we become; and the more motivated we become, the more likely we are to accomplish our goal.

This "in for a penny, in for a pound" formula also explains why venture capitalists expect budding entrepreneurs to have lots of financial "skin in the game" before they invest themselves. In effect, the more you invest, the more invested you become, and the harder it is to quit and write off your investment.

Of course, no "formula" is perfect. At times even the motivational power of sacrifice can lead to negative outcomes. In business, as in our personal lives, we are often reluctant to give up on failed strategies precisely because we are so invested in them. In business these investments of time, energy, and money are called "sunk costs," and our tendency to let these prior investments bias our current decisions can lead to disaster. Investors often irrationally refuse to sell at a loss, and many corporations inflexibly resist writing off a failing business that is clearly a drain on resources that would be better deployed elsewhere. In these cases our investments of time and money often result in "throwing good money after bad" in the vain hope that our previous sacrifices may be made whole.

There is no simple answer to this age-old poker conundrum of knowing when to hold 'em and when to fold 'em, but the monastic tradition of "excellence for its own sake" offers a few guidelines.

Returning to chapter 5, the first lesson is having a big enough mission. If your mission is making white widgets, then it will be very hard to admit that it is time to take your lumps and start making black ones. On the other hand, if, like the monks and Truliant Federal Credit Union, your mission is delighting customers, then reinventing your business will be far easier. If your mission is becoming an individual or business that values excellence, then learning how to make painful decisions despite sunk costs will inevitably be part of your curriculum. No matter how much you sacrifice for excellence, you will never have to worry about your investment leading you astray.

In a later chapter, we shall see that the monks of Mepkin faced just such a painful decision when they abandoned their beloved egg business and transitioned into mushrooms instead. This decision meant writing off a lot of plant, equipment, and know-how, and embarking on a long and painful transformation that only now—after several years of backpedaling in the Desert—is starting to pay off. The key to their successful transformation is that there is nothing in Mepkin's mission about eggs per se. The monk's passion for excellence is not focused on a product or even a business model. The monastic mission is focused on a way of doing business rather than a specific business. Aiming past the target of business made a difficult business decision for the monks far less traumatic.

The second tip for managing the inevitable tension between determination and masochism is the monastic virtue of discernment. The monks spend hours each day in contemplation, and, as we noted previously, much of this contemplation is dedicated to discerning what is true from what only seems to be true. Again, aim past the target: if a big part of your personal and organizational mission is learning how to make better decisions, it is impossible to become too addicted to your mission.

Detachment is the third monastic virtue that will keep you from protecting sunk cost investments at the expense of better opportunities. Later we will discuss this monastic business virtue in depth, but for now it is important to remember that detachment is not the opposite of passionate commitment. The opposite of detachment is *identification*. It is the dangers inherent in emotional identification that are captured so well in the Wall Street caveat: "Never fall in love with a stock."

The lesson from the monks is simple: the more you focus on principles, values, and virtues rather than specific stocks, products, and services, the more likely it is that you will make the right decisions *about* specific stocks, products, and services. Truliant, for example, is fanatically investing in building a culture of customer service. As a result, Truliant is far more open to the constantly changing demands of the marketplace than a company focused merely on making a profit would be. And it is extremely hard to imagine how Truliant's investment could ever become a sunk cost that should be written off. Great business decisions for the monks and companies like Truliant are the by-product of a culture based on the right values.

Creating a spirit of shared sacrifice is also critical to overcoming the decline in employee engagement and corporate loyalty that we noted earlier. Establishing this spirit depends on articulating a mission worthy of being served and using it to tap into the innate human longing for something worth sacrificing for, a heroic impulse we have been calling the urge to transformation. Sacrifice in this context often eventually transcends its painful and even onerous connotations. Hitting the gym may start as a painful sacrifice, but over time it often becomes fun.

Samuel Johnson once said that the knowledge of one's imminent execution wonderfully focuses the mind. The same might be said of anything we truly sacrifice for. The more a company invests in excellence, the more committed to excellence it becomes, until one day it becomes an excellent company. This is exactly the approach that Jack Welch took at General Electric in the 1980s and 1990s. Welch fanatically focused on building a culture of quality and excellence until he had transformed GE from a tired old relic of the Industrial Age into one of the fastest-growing and most admired corporations in the world. Under Welch none of GE's products or business units ever became too sacred to reinvent or exit. The only thing that was sacred was the spirit of excellence itself. As *USA Today* said about the beer-brewing monks of St. Sixtus, Welch was prepared to break every business rule in the book except a commitment to quality.

$$\bigcirc$$

THE BUSINESS SUCCESS of Mepkin Abbey relies on its reputation for providing only products of the highest quality. For weeks on end, I've worked the "round table," the last step in the grading process, stuffing egg cartons into Father Malachy's boxes according to size. The conveyor constantly spitting cartons onto the spinning table makes for a whirlwind of a job—a job that Father Christian says "tends to engender panic." I had to labor mightily just to stay a carton or two ahead of that stubborn wheel and its spiteful predilection for spewing perfectly good eggs onto the floor if it thought I wasn't paying it enough attention. I usually succeeded, but on the one occasion that I did not, Brother John only smiled at my sheepish expression and said, "Don't worry about it. It's in the nature of eggs to break." Then he helped me clean up the mess.

Every once in a while, Father Stan, Mepkin's cellarer, or business manager, at the time, would wander by and gently remind me that I was the last bastion of quality control before the eggs went off to market. There was no need to remind me—I don't think I've ever taken any job more seriously. Despite my incipient panic, I scanned each carton with eye and hand for the occasional cracked egg. And when I discovered one, I would set the carton aside with the satisfied sense that I had just singlehandedly saved humanity from imminent catastrophe.

At every stage of Mepkin's business, quality is paramount, and a prayerful attitude prevails not only for products but in the way the food is prepared, the laundry washed, and the guesthouses cleaned and arranged for the next sojourning retreatant.

But even though anyone on the line could shut down the egg conveyor when quality was threatened, product quality was not the point. Mepkin's fanatical commitment to quality is just the by-product of living life with a prayerful attitude. Excellence for the sake of excellence is what really motivates the monks and drives their monastic businesses. Every time I am tempted to cut a corner or fall back on a "that's good enough" attitude, I am reminded of why I go to Mepkin in the first place and "offer it up" instead. After all, why bother to make the sacrifice of getting up at three A.M. to pray if I'm just going to goof off at work?

But the excellence for the sake of excellence attitude that the monks evince emerges from something even deeper. All too often we compartmentalize our work, personal, and spiritual lives. We erect "Chinese walls" between them, leading to contradictions that border on hypocrisy. For the monks these walls do not exist. They live cheek by jowl, and the professional, personal, organizational, and spiritual are all one. For a monk, being on time for work is not just part of his job description. It is a discipline that personally builds willpower, that organizationally offers efficiency, and that spiritually offers the compassion to his brothers and customers that he prays God and others will extend to him.

The secret to the monks' success is not that they have managed to establish the mythical "healthy balance" between their personal and professional lives. The secret is that their personal, organizational, and business lives are all subsets of their one, high, over-arching mission—becoming the best human beings they can possibly be. Like Brother Joseph, the monks have learned to "offer up" everything they do.

⬭

AS I MENTIONED PREVIOUSLY, Father Francis Kline, besides being one of the most impressive leaders I have ever met, also happened to be a Juilliard-trained organist who, much to the disappointment of the *New York Times,* gave up a lucrative recording contract and certain stardom to enter a Trappist monastery. One day, Meredith Parker, then president of the Duke University chapter of the SKS, told me that she and her fellow students wanted to invite Father Francis to give an organ recital at the Duke Chapel entitled *Spiritual Bach.*

Though I doubted that Francis would accept an invitation to leave the monastery, I was moved by her audacity, so I encouraged her to give it a try. After all, learning that the impossible is often possible was one of the things that the SKS was all about.

So I was thrilled when her invitation enticed Francis to leave the cloister for one of his exceedingly rare organ recitals. But as I walked him toward the main entrance to the Duke Chapel, neither of us was prepared for what we saw.

It was the kind of mob scene usually reserved for rock concerts and Final Four basketball games. Hundreds of people crowded the door as local television stations filmed it all. Amazed and a trifle alarmed, I lowered my head and shouldered Francis into the chapel. As he made his way to the organ loft, Will Willimon, the dean of the Duke Chapel and the faculty advisor of the SKS, appeared at my side. "I've never seen anything like it," he said. "I told the students not to get their hopes up. I told them that if they got 50 folks for a free organ recital, they'd be doing great. This place holds 1,800 without the sanctuary, and we'll be lucky to get them all in standing room only. And at twenty bucks a head?" Then he added with a grin, "I guess I'll never live it down with the kids."

Then he introduced me to the chapel's organist before scurrying off to open the choir seats bordering the sanctuary for the overflowing crowd. The organist pumped my hand and said with real excitement, "We've never pulled a crowd for an organ recital before. I guess this just shows what a little advertising will do!"

I knew better. I knew that no money whatsoever was spent on advertising. Instead I was witnessing the fruits of a grassroots effort by a tireless bunch of students and a handful of adults from our Friday group who had volunteered their expertise. Over the last several months, I'd watched in awe as meeting after meeting left students—already saddled with a full load of courses—loaded down with work that would make highly paid employees blanch.

Press releases appeared in almost every newspaper in North Carolina; fliers were handed out at local churches; all over the Duke campus, tables were manned by eager student ticket sellers; advertising in the program was sold to local merchants; classical radio stations incessantly plugged the recital; and television stations were convinced to cover the event. Many students stepped up and bought 20 or 25 tickets with a "sell 'em or eat 'em" attitude. I was looking at so much more than "a little advertising."

Catching my breath, I looked around at the brimming crowd and noticed 10 or 12 student ushers taking it all in stride: young college men in jackets and ties and young college women in dresses, each armed with a walkie-talkie, knowing his or her job, and quietly doing it. Then I saw Meredith, the focal point for all this activity. I watched her calmly directing traffic from her walkie-talkie. Eventually she caught my eye and gave me a reassuring smile that said: "Relax, why don't you? We got it." And I relaxed.

When the recital started, more than two thousand people were in the Duke Chapel, and almost all had seats. Francis received two standing ovations and rave reviews. Brother Joshua told me later that Francis told him: "A packed house, an incredible organ, and Bach. All I can say is, I gave the best I have to give. I played my heart out." He certainly did—and so did the students of the SKS.

So what motivated these students to promote an organ recital as if they were climbing Mount Everest? Obviously it was not money, stock options, or a chance for advancement. It definitely didn't arise from a newfound affinity for classical music. And though the proceeds went to charity, I don't think the answer lies in community service either.

Instead the catalyst was a desire to do something excellently for nothing more than its own reward. An organ recital was just an opportunity to take all the principles concerning the Hero's Journey and self-transcendence that we discussed in our weekly meetings and put them to the test in real time under the pressure of real-world constraints. It was merely a way for the students to stretch, leave their comfort zone, and find out by doing that most of our constraints are self-imposed. As with RGI, it was a way to discover firsthand what a group of committed individuals could become by working together on a worthwhile mission. Above all, *Spiritual Bach* lives on in my own memory as an example of the passion that can be produced when ordinary people sense a goat-rodeo opportunity for a transformation of *being*.

Several months after Francis's organ recital, the students designed a T-shirt to commemorate the event. On the back of the T-shirt, they stenciled this quote from an anonymous source:

Watch your thoughts for they become your actions.
Watch your actions because they become your habits.
Watch your habits because they become your character.
Watch your character because it becomes your destiny.

The T-shirts sold out in a matter of days. When I took the students to Mepkin on a retreat, they presented one to Father Christian. He responded to the quote on the back by saying, "That's all you need to know," and he wore his T-shirt over his habit for the balance of their stay.

Over time a number of SKS students joined our company, usually as sales reps, after graduation. At first this was greeted with alarm by a sales director we had recruited from outside our community. The kids didn't have any sales experience—or any business experience at all, for that matter. Besides, he felt that my partners and I were merely showing favoritism for a pet project.

Then, about a year later, he came into my office. "By the way," he said, "do you think we can get any more of those SKS kids? They don't care about money, and frankly I don't have a clue about what drives them. But they're honest, dependable, and work their tails off. They're the best employees we have."

He was a great employee himself, but he never did understand what turned those kids into passionately engaged employees. Over the years many SKS students on the verge of graduation told me the same thing, with the air of someone making a remarkable discovery for the very first time: "You know, I never would've believed it, but I got so much more out of putting on events than I ever got from attending the events themselves." Like Brother Joseph and Jack Welch, they had come to understand that excellence is its own reward. But they only arrived at this magical understanding by having enough faith to give Confucius a real-world try: "I hear and I forget. I see and I remember. I do and I understand."

A Corporate Case Study

LOUIS R. MOBLEY INSISTED that great leaders and great organizations are distinguished not by their skills but by their values. Instilling a value like excellence for the sake of excellence is not something that can be done in a class. In fact one of Mobley's most important discoveries was that values change only through experience, and that is why the IBM Executive School dispensed with podiums and textbooks in favor of a completely experiential curriculum. But despite the success of his school, Mobley always believed that the best way to change values was on the job, through changing the experience of the workplace. Once again it is culture that matters most. So how do you instill excellence for the sake of excellence into a secular organization? In the late 1980s, I was confronted with just this challenge.

I was working as a consultant for a Washington, DC–based company called Data Broadcasting Corporation (DBC) when the CEO asked to see me. He was unhappy with the results that the sales department was generating under the current vice president of sales and asked me to take the job. I was intrigued by the opportunity. Though we had never spoken of it before, my own analysis matched the CEO's.

Long before the Internet, DBC's *MarketWatch* offered real-time stock quotes to self-employed day traders and stock market fanatics via their home PCs. Data Broadcasting Corporation was a subsidiary of the Financial News Network (FNN), and television advertising on FNN generated mountains of leads in the form of inbound, toll-free telephone calls. Besides, *MarketWatch* was a subscription product producing the holy grail of business: recurring revenue.

But despite a great product, an abundance of leads, recurring revenue, and a more than generous compensation package for the sales force, revenue was anemic and, worse still, flat. The 25 sales reps who manned the phones seemed to be merely going through the motions, coming in late and leaving early. Their attitude reminded me of a *MAD* magazine poster with Alfred E. Neuman grinning away above the caption, "What, me worry?" Meanwhile the current vice president of sales seemed more interested in being their friend than their leader.

But though I was excited by the challenge of changing this culture, I told the CEO that there was a problem. I was chairing an SKS meeting on Thursdays at North Carolina State University as well as our adult group on Fridays, so I could only be on site three days a week.

"That's all right," the CEO growled. "I'm convinced you'll get more done in three days than we're getting now in five."

Some years ago I read a story in the *Wall Street Journal* about the man who turned around the New York City subway system. As someone who had experienced the abominable subway conditions that prevailed prior to his arrival, I eagerly read the article. Despite the myriad and seemingly intractable problems he inherited, the first thing he did was concentrate on eliminating graffiti from the trains. Every time a train finished its run, it was repainted and sent back out, robbing the graffiti artists of the chance to savor their work. Demoralized, they soon gave up.

But there was more to it than cleaning up trains. Breaking the back of graffiti was a brilliant symbolic move. In a stroke it dramatically signaled to employees and consumers alike that there was a new sheriff in town: a sheriff who would no longer tolerate the pathos and mediocrity of business as usual. Rather than squander his political capital on issues that would take years to accomplish, he chose a highly visible symbolic move that offered the chance for a quick and decisive victory: a victory that instantly provided the confidence and leverage he needed to take an even larger step. Over time, he repeated this process of leveraging victories into bigger goals and bigger victories until, little by little, he transformed the New York City subway system.

I used the same approach at DBC. The very next day, I showed up two hours early in order to make sure that I was the first arrival. As each sales rep arrived, I affably introduced myself as the new vice president of sales. This continued until nine A.M. After that each arrival got the same treatment with two additional words: "You're late."

The next day I did the same, and only a couple of reps were late. On the third day, mirabile dictu, every rep came to work on time. Meanwhile, during the day I barely frequented my office. I tried to be everywhere at once, asking questions, offering encouragement, and probing into policies and procedures that, while mostly sound, had long been honored more in the breach than the observance.

I gave each sales rep a binder, and when I reminded them that it was company policy, for example, that each rep be in his or her seat ready to sell when a commercial ran on FNN, I dashed to my office, wrote a memo to this effect, and instructed them to add it to their binder. Little by little I created a manual that left no room for ambiguity.

When they complained that it was hard to remember when the ads were running, I erected a whiteboard with the schedule and updated it daily. I listened carefully to their feedback and eliminated useless or counterproductive policies, but I told them that from then on, there would be no excuses for a failure to abide by any company policy that had survived our pruning. The reps were now accountable for these specific policies, but, more importantly, I used this manual to signal a new culture of accountability.

During this time I made no speeches. Nor did I make any threats. I concentrated on demonstrating that I was going to lead from the front and work harder than anyone, and that the mediocrity of business as usual would no longer be tolerated. Neither tardiness nor policies were my primary concern. They were merely symbolic proxies I used to focus on my real concern: a lackadaisical attitude. I even walked fast and talked even faster in order to demonstrate the urgent tempo I expected to see in them. Though I never mentioned sales production, we experienced a small but noticeable bump in sales during those first few days.

The following Monday I arrived at our first formal meeting wearing a cowboy hat. I told them that I was so pleased by our progress that I was introducing a contest. But first I told them a story.

"My friend Pat Grotto," I told them, "is the most colorful person and the best salesman that I've ever met. He is also the only six-foot-three, 220-pound Italian I've ever seen. One day he said to me, 'Augs, what am I supposed to do? I got this reputation as the fastest sales gun in the West, and it follows me wherever I go. All these young sales punks keep coming around wanting to take me on. They wanna draw on me. Why? Why? You know me, Augs, you know I'm a man of peace with a heart of gold. All I wanna do is hang up my six-shooters, buy a farm, and grow lima beans. But these young guns won't leave me alone. I beg them, plead with them. Look at these hands! They're covered with blood! I'm begging you, I tell them, don't do it, don't draw on me!'

"Then his lips curled, his black eyes flashed, and he hissed through his teeth, 'But they won't listen. They never listen. They gotta know . . . they gotta know . . . they go for their gun AND I SHOOT 'EM DOWN LIKE A DOG!' "

Mimicking Pat, I concluded his story at the top of my lungs, which had the desired effect of reducing the tension with humor while building it for what might be coming next. I told them that in a few moments, I was going to throw my cowboy hat into the middle of the table. One person would pick it up and put it on his head. This gesture would serve notice on the rest of the team that he was, like Pat Grotto, the fastest sales gun in the West.

This gunslinger would then approach each of the other reps individually and beg them not to "draw" on him. Each rep in turn would then have the option of either accepting or rejecting this face-to-face challenge. If the fastest gun succeeded in shooting all his challengers "down like a dog," he would get $500 in cash. Any challenger who outsold the gunslinger would get $50.

But before throwing my hat onto the table, I added one more twist. Until now the sales procedure had been to field incoming calls for *MarketWatch* with little effort to close on the first call. Instead literature and a demo would be sent out, and the reps would wait for the prospect to call back and place an order.

I knew that a prospect, especially one motivated enough to pick up a phone, is most excited by a product or service the first time he hears about it. As a result my little twist was that only sales made on a "one call, one close, one credit card" basis would count toward the contest. Then I threw the hat onto the table. . . .

All eyes were glued to the hat, but no one moved or said a word. The silence became deafening, and still no one moved. What would I do if no one picked up the hat? The loss of face would be so devastating I might never recover.

Suddenly Scott Wilkes grabbed the hat and put it on his head. Then he confronted every member of the team and each one, despite his threat to shoot them down, accepted his challenge.

Minutes later the phones started ringing and the reps started selling like the fate of the world hung in the balance. But though I was relieved by their reaction, I was worried about my hired gun.

Scott, a high-school-educated former tree pruner, was the last person I'd expected to pick up my hat. His numbers were poor, and he seemed to lack the sophistication and people skills that sales requires. His underdog status, coupled to the courage it took to pick up my hat, had won my heart—not to mention that this former tree climber had quite possibly saved my butt.

But at the end of the first day, Scott was on top, despite the fact that sales had exploded. It was the same the second day. On the third day, I wandered by the sales pit just as an FNN commercial was winding up and the phones were beginning to ring. Oblivious to my presence, Scott leaped to his feet and screamed at the receptionist routing the calls, "Gimme a call! For God's sake, gimme a call!" He got his call from the shell-shocked receptionist and quickly signed up a new customer. Then he noticed me grinning at him from ear to ear.

"Yeah, yeah," he said, wildly grinning back. "That look in your eyes. My wife says I got that crazy look now, too!"

Scott handily won the contest, and I don't think I was ever happier for another human being. But it didn't end there. Over the ensuing weeks and months—despite the fact that the extra monetary incentive was no longer in place—Scott was consistently our number one or number two rep. Unable to account for his performance by skills alone, I finally stopped by his desk and asked him about it. Why, I asked, had he gone from dead last to a consistent top performer in the space of a single week?

"It's simple, Augie," he said, peering up at me through his thick glasses. "Once you know what it feels like to be your best, you never, *ever* want to go back."

All I could do was extend my arm and silently shake his hand.

That one-week contest was a transformational inflection point. No one wanted to go back. Even though there were no more special incentives, sales doubled, then tripled, then quadrupled. Meanwhile the spirit of excellence gradually spread to other departments, until we were all sprinting ahead in lockstep. Everyone was working 10 times harder and having a thousand times more fun. Every week I flew to Raleigh for my meetings and returned on Sunday, leaving one of the reps in charge. They received no additional compensation for their managerial chores, but the reps competed for the job, and sales actually went up while I was away.

I was so amazed by this phenomenon that I decided to stick my neck out yet again. After two quarters of spectacular growth, I decided to turn over complete control to the sales force for the final quarter of DBC's fiscal year, coinciding with Christmas. As soon as I made my announcement, everyone in sales, including our administrative staff, disappeared into a conference room. They emerged with several elected "captains" tasked with setting our fourth-quarter goal and making it happen. Their goal was so aggressive that I was tempted to intervene for fear that they were setting themselves up for a letdown. But I had given my word, so all I could do was step back and watch.

For three months I sat on my hands in a purely consultative role—the hardest job I've ever had. With two weeks to go in the quarter, it was unclear that they would make it. There was nothing I could do except gnaw my fingernails down to the second knuckle and pray. Then, with a final surge, in the final week, right down to the final hour, they blew through their "impossible" goal.

I found out later that in those final days, the reps gave away their commissions to prospective customers as discounts in order to reach their goal. I insisted that the company reimburse them. (The captain behind this selfless stratagem was a twenty-two-year-old college dropout, selling machine, and emerging leader named Jay Hall—my future partner at RGI.)

In celebration we threw a huge New Year's bash for the whole company. During the party, one of our programmers approached me. He was already deep in his cups.

"Listen," he said slurring his words ever so slightly, "sales are up five times in nine months. What's the secret?"

Taking into account his engineering mindset as well as his current condition, I simply said, "They wanted it."

He furrowed his brow and shook his head. "I don't get it. Product's the same, price's the same, leads are the same, and the people are the same. Hell, even the commissions are the same. Didn't they want it before?"

"Yeah, they wanted it before. But they really want it now."

Giving it up for a bad job, he merely shook his head and went back for another drink.

Perhaps I took advantage of his inebriation, but I honestly couldn't think of a way to convey it in the 25 words or less that he expected. He wanted a technique, and all I had to offer was a way of life. The "secret" was that, just like the monks, through lots of mostly little things, I had tapped into the universal human longing for transformation. In effect I didn't do anything. I just allowed something always there waiting to happen to actually happen. Our final-quarter results, for example, relied on my willingness to surrender control, or, as the monks would say, "Let go and let God."

Scott Wilkes said it best. Once we know what excellence for the sake of excellence feels like, we never want to go back. Leadership's job is to set the expectations and establish the conditions for this transformational experience to take place. Most important, it is leadership's job to set the example. As my friend at Microsoft said, it's all about goat rodeos.

Scott Wilkes eventually left DBC and relocated with his family to California. Last I heard he had a couple of kids, had been promoted many times, and was making $300,000 a year. Not bad for a high school grad in his early thirties, back in the early 1990s, who barely a year before we met had been climbing trees for minimum wage.

◯

INCULCATING A VALUE like excellence for the sake of excellence is as much art as science, but careful examination of the DBC case study reveals a number of lessons.

1. *Human beings are symbolic creatures.* As Carl Jung pointed out in his seminal *Psyche and Symbol,* almost everything in life is symbolic of something deeper. Even words are symbols. Almost everything I did at DBC was symbolic; even the prize money I offered in the gunslinger contest was mostly symbolic. It is no accident that Trappist monks are surrounded by meaningful symbols.

2. *Don't trade voice for leg.* My father always said that the number one mistake that parents make with young children is trading voice for leg. I didn't just tell the reps to be on time, I showed them, by arriving for work two hours early. Never lecture. Act.

3. *Seize the initiative.* Perceptions are reality, and nothing creates the perception of change like moving rapidly. Remember what my boss and mentor Jim Collins told me: "Augie, when you take a new job or assignment, hire somebody, fire somebody, rearrange the furniture, but whatever you do, do it fast!"

4. *Focus, focus, focus.* While it may have appeared that I was doing a thousand things at once, I was focused on only one thing: creating a culture of excellence. Even sales numbers rarely crossed my mind except as a barometer for how well I was changing the culture. In the end it wasn't about money. If it had been, the reps would not have given away their commissions to reach their collective goal.

5. *Follow up, follow up, follow up.* I gradually changed hundreds of things at DBC, but I never introduced a change unless I

had the time to ruthlessly follow it up. I followed up until the behavioral change had become so habitual and automatic that I only had to check on it once in a while. By following up on even the smallest things, I demonstrated that excellence must be the norm, not the exception.

6. *Take risks.* My fast-gun contest and my decision to let the reps run sales were fraught with risk. But if I wasn't ready to take risks, how could I expect people like Scott Wilkes and Jay Hall to take them? The Hero's Journey is a risky business, and without risk, there is no progress. Besides, what fun is a riskless adventure?

7. *Shatter the glass box.* Every individual, department, or company eventually encloses itself in a glass box: a box of assumptions about what is possible. For the longest time, breaking the four-minute mile was considered impossible. But when Roger Bannister broke this barrier, within months, many did. The same holds true in business. Find an individual or department eager for change and focus on them until this glass box has been broken. Everyone else will then follow. The one-time contest at DBC was designed to perform this function. By smashing the box, Scott Wilkes demonstrated that anyone could, and this inspirational jolt was crucial to changing the culture.

8. *Don't change everything at once.* Focus small, get a quick victory, turn it into a well-oiled template, and only then roll it out. Every change I made at DBC was initially provisional. For the first week or so, I would manage it intensively, looking for the consequences I had failed to consider during the planning process. Once I got all the feedback I needed, I would redesign the change if necessary and only then "go live" with it.

9. *You gotta care.* None of these measures amount to a tinker's damn unless you care deeply about people. I may have come across as the adult authority figure, but I cared deeply about all the people at DBC, and they responded in kind. When I left DBC, one of the reps asked to see me. "Augie, you are the biggest pain in the ass I've ever met," she said, "but never in my wildest dreams did I

ever imagine I could be this successful. Why did you care so much about me?"

10. *It's all about the mission.* Money played its role at DBC, but mostly as a symbol pointing at something much larger: the mission and the opportunity for transformation this mission represented. It was not that Jay Hall was such a great salesman or leader that drew me to him. His willingness to forgo his own commissions and convince others to follow his lead showed that he was able to put the mission, the good of the whole, ahead of his own selfish desires. It was his service-and-selflessness attitude that made him someone I wanted as a future partner and lifelong friend.

8

ETHICAL STANDARDS, OR, WHY GOOD THINGS HAPPEN FOR GOOD PEOPLE

I CONFESS that when I am living at Mepkin Abbey, I take pride in thinking of myself as something of a "go-to guy" for the monks. It gives me great satisfaction when Brother John asks me to help Father Guerric put up Christmas trees or to aid Brother Hugh as he feeds huge oak logs into the oversized wood-burning furnace that heats the church. I also try to pitch in unasked by wiping out a refrigerator once in a while, and I think I won Brother Edward's heart by occasionally surprising him with a freshly mopped floor when he returned to his kitchen duties after his midday siesta— even though the first time I did so, I used so much pine-scented cleaning solution that I did a better job clearing the refectory of monks than clearing the floor of dirt.

Besides prayer, there is nothing closer to the Trappist heart than work—Brother Nick told me that people in France still use the expression, "getting as dirty as a Trappist" to describe a hard day's work. Nothing makes me feel closer to the heartbeat of Mepkin than when Brother John, naturally and without reluctance, asks me to do some extra work around the monastery. It is perhaps the closest I ever come to feeling like a member of the community.

Father Stan is now Mepkin's abbot, but when I met him in 1996, he was Mepkin's cellarer, or business manager. One evening, just after the last monastic service, Father Stan whispered that he wanted me to meet him at his office just after Vigils at four A.M. When I arrived, we jumped into his golf cart and headed out through a dark, chilly morning to the grading house, where we rapidly loaded the monastery's delivery truck with cartons of refrigerated eggs. When we finished, he asked me to accompany him as his helper later that morning as he made his deliveries.

Father Stan is a youthful and solidly built man with a closely cropped beard that matches the closely cropped hair that surrounds his balding head. Affable and even-tempered, Stan always maintained an air of easygoing competence: a guy who knew what he was doing and was quietly getting on with it. Stan also struck me agreeably as a "man's man" or "regular guy," an impression that was only reinforced by the solicitous way in which he treated the young women that I brought to Mepkin as part of an SKS student retreat—even inviting the ladies to the grading house so they could see how the eggs were processed despite the "Monastery Only" sign that stands guard over the road leading to the eggery.

But despite the self-deprecating sense of humor that led him to doff his hat from his bald head as we raced along in the golf cart and say, "I love to feel the wind in my hair," Stan is deadly serious about his monastic vocation.

Stan entered Mepkin as a postulant within days of graduating from high school. At the going-away party thrown by his friends before he left, he ate as much watermelon as he could stomach because he was convinced that he would never eat his favorite food again. His family was so devastated by his decision to become a monk that his father refused to speak to him for years. In light of these revelations, I asked him if he had any regrets.

"Yeah," he said with a grin. "I should've joined sooner."

Later that morning, as we headed out through the monastery gates with Stan at the wheel of a truckload of eggs, I remembered this remark when I noticed him fingering his rosary beads. What for me was a chance to hit the road and see the sights, for Stan was just a chance to squeeze in some extra prayer.

But what really impressed me about that trip was the way in which Stan was greeted at every grocery store we visited. Far from being treated like just another vendor, he was welcomed like one of the family. It was clear that, just as I get a feeling of belonging by taking on extra work at the monastery, all the grocery store personnel considered it a privilege to be able to market Mepkin's eggs—a privilege that gave them a warm feeling, however tenuous, of being connected to something bigger and nobler than themselves.

Then, at one of the stores, we ran into one of the chain's buyers. The man buttonholed Stan and made his case for marketing Mepkin's eggs as a premium product at a substantially higher price than the eggs he bought from his other vendors. Stan listened patiently and thanked the man for his kindness (the buyer didn't want any of the price increase for himself), but, he said, "an egg is an egg," and the brothers in good conscience couldn't justify charging more than the prevailing price. The buyer was amazed, and so was I. Never in my business career had one of my distributors pleaded for a higher price.

○

ALTHOUGH STAN'S DECISION was injurious to Mepkin's bottom line in the short run, in the long run, it was beneficial. Despite his disappointment, I could see that the buyer was impressed, and no business I know of has ever had a better and more loyal distribution system than Mepkin Abbey. Again and again I've seen grocers, caterers, and bakers go the extra mile to make sure that Mepkin's eggs had a market.

A reputation for honesty and integrity is one of those "intangible assets" that pays off in ways we can never fully anticipate. It is Mepkin's commitment to its core principles that makes ethical decisions easy even when the pressure is on.

Once the monastery ran short of eggs, and Father Stan had to buy some from another distributor in order to fill his orders. Despite the fact that a hard deadline was looming and the pressure was becoming intense, Stan insisted that we open every carton and regrade every egg in order to make sure that these eggs, like all Mepkin's eggs, met his exacting standards for quality. I was amazed at how many cracked and imperfect eggs we ended up rejecting. Mepkin definitely lost money on that deal.

While we often think that unethical behavior is the result of bad people doing bad things, it actually usually arises from good people doing bad things from fear and insecurity. At Mepkin the monks are rooted in a tradition that transcends the kind of every-man-for-himself mentality that so often leads to unethical behavior under pressure. Besides the obvious role that religious morality plays, there are three additional aspects of monastic formation that lead to an ethical attitude toward business that we can all learn to emulate.

First is a long-term attitude. In contrast to our fixation on quarterly profits, the monks are in it for the long haul. I asked Brother Robert one time how long it had been since Father Anthony, Mepkin's first abbot, had died. "Five or six years," he replied. I told him that was impossible, since I had only been coming to Mepkin for three years and Father Anthony had been alive when I first arrived.

"Three years, five years, ten, eternity," he replied with a grin, "it's all the same to us. We're Trappists. There's no time here."

This timeless attitude leads to a strong sense of deferred gratification. Again, ethical behavior is something that pays off in the long run. It is often our penchant for expediency and instant gratification that lead us to take the ethical shortcuts that can ruin a business, a reputation, or even a life.

The second Trappist secret to maintaining only the highest ethical standards is detachment. Detachment is a monastic virtue that is often misunderstood. As we noted briefly in chapter 7, we usually think of detachment as the cold, bloodless opposite of passion and commitment. The opposite of detachment, however, is not passionate commitment; it is *identification*. Being able to identify with the characters in a movie—what psychologists call "a willing suspension of disbelief"—is essential to enjoying a film, but it is often disastrous in the rest of our lives. A person who identifies with a new couch experiences a sense of personal loss when someone spills something on it. This person no longer *owns* a couch; he has, in a sense, *become* the couch. Similarly, we can become so identified with our job and title that if either is threatened, we react with the kind of fear that is only appropriate to life-threatening situations.

In 2002 three of my brothers drove their snowmobiles off a cliff amidst whiteout conditions in Vail, Colorado. My brother Jamie was killed, and my brothers Dan and Tom, seriously injured, were stranded on the mountain all night in −40-degree temperatures and −60-degree windchill, until they were finally rescued. Two of the rescue workers were hospitalized with frostbite, and Tom eventually lost some pieces of his toes.

Two years later my brother Dan, an executive with a major media company, told me that one of his sales directors had recently called, terrified that the rumors circulating about layoffs might be true and that she might be laid off.

The woman was almost hysterical, and despite Dan's repeated assurances that he knew no more than she did, she refused to be mollified.

"But you don't understand," she insisted. "I have three kids, I can't afford to be laid off."

"Listen, Anne," Dan told her, "I don't know anything more than you do. Hell, maybe I'll be laid off, and I got kids, too. But I do know this: This is not the end of the world. I've been to the end of the world, and this is not it."

The next day the woman called back in tears. She had told her husband what Dan had said, and now all she wanted to do was thank him for reminding them both of how lucky they really were.

Despite the horror of the accident, Dan emerged with a monklike detachment that allowed him to keep things in perspective. His detachment isn't a passionless obstacle; it is a virtue that allows him to make clear business choices unfettered by the fearful identifications that so often lead to poor and unethical decisions. Dan has been extremely successful in his career since the accident, and according to him this is because his co-workers and clients now trust him more than ever to always "play it straight" and "do the right thing."

I will never forget arriving in Denver's Stapleton airport the day after the accident with my father and my brother Jon. We were greeted by newspaper headlines about my brothers throughout the airport. Only a last-minute cancelation had spared me from sharing my brothers' fate, and for months I nursed my brother and closest friend, Tom, as he suffered with broken ribs and vertebrae and repeatedly had to return to the burn unit for the excruciating surgeries that managed to save his foot and most of his blackened toes. This experience reminded me, too, of what is really important, and I rededicated myself to my family and my spiritual vocation as a result.

Detachment doesn't mean rootless laziness. It means being rooted in something much bigger than ourselves, something that transcends our narrow personal concerns. As I mentioned in a prior chapter, it was my own detachment that allowed me to turn down a job at UPI in order to avoid breaking my promise to help some college kids. It was detachment that made it possible for me to keep my commitment to attending my meetings in Raleigh, even if it meant passing up the offer to work full time at DBC. By being rooted in something I considered more important than business, I was successfully able to resist the temptation to use rationalization to unethically break my promises in exchange for a monetary reward.

Besides, if I hadn't insisted on attending my meetings, I never would have left a sales rep in charge while I was absent from DBC. It was this "accident" that led me to letting the reps run the show and to our spectacular fourth-quarter numbers at DBC. Rather than a business obstacle, the detachment that allowed me to remain true to my ethical obligations led to amazing results at DBC that I never could have predicted.

The third monastic secret to ethical behavior is, once again, aiming past the target. In previous chapters I applied this concept to creating organizational and personal missions, but it applies just as well to making ethical decisions. Our monomaniacal obsession with quarterly earnings is a great example of the negative consequences that transpire when we fail to aim past the target. Warren Buffett, in his annual letter to shareholders, constantly inveighs against this kind of short-term thinking. Every year he reminds his shareholders that Berkshire Hathaway is in it for the long haul—just as the monks are—and it is not an accident that his long-term thinking is bound up with his reputation for only the highest ethical behavior.

As we noted in the first chapter, people like Trappist monks and Buffett are not successful despite their high ethical ideals, but because of them. Of course I would argue that there is a target to aim at that surpasses even the long-term financial health of a company like Berkshire Hathaway. If you want to be successful, you must be ethical. If you want to be ethical, you must be detached. You cultivate detachment by rooting yourself in something bigger than yourself and your personal concerns. Whether you take it literally or metaphorically, seek first the kingdom of heaven and everything else will take care of itself—including business.

IN THE FALL of 1999, Lev Zaidenberg, the CEO of an Israeli company called Mutek, walked into my office. Raleigh Group

International had rapidly become Mutek's largest American distributor, and Lev was making a two-hour detour on his way from New York City to Silicon Valley in order to try to persuade us to sell even more of his product. But as I rose to shake his hand, he glanced at a book on my desk. "Wow," he said, "you're reading Chekhov." I told him that I had graduated with a degree in Russian History and that this had led to my lifelong passion for Russian literature, including Chekhov.

"But I am Russian!" he exclaimed, and he told me that he had been one of the famous Jewish "refusniks" back in the 1970s, who at great personal risk had stood up to the Soviet regime. After many trials at the hands of the KGB, he had finally been granted permission to emigrate to Israel.

In response I repeated my previous greeting, but this time in Russian. We fell into an animated conversation (mercifully, in English) about Russian history, literature, and spirituality. Two hours later I volunteered to drive my new best friend back to the airport so we could continue our conversation. At the terminal he looked at me and smiled. "You know, we didn't get any business done."

He suggested that I meet him in New York City in a week so that we could hammer out a deal. A week later, I walked into his hotel suite, and for the next four hours, we continued our previous conversation around issues that, Lev said, in Russia require a full liter of vodka to really address. Finally he leaned back in his chair with his hands behind his neck and laughed out loud.

"You know," he said, "we still have not mentioned a word about business. I have a better idea. Why don't we just buy your company?"

Two weeks later my partners and I arrived in Tel Aviv, Israel, and despite Lev's lavish hospitality, which took us to Jerusalem and all the holy sites, during our visit we managed to sign the preliminary paperwork that set the wheels of an acquisition in motion.

And then all hell broke loose. Lawyers and accountants from Tel Aviv, New York, and North Carolina converged on our offices to do due diligence and all the other million and one things that must be done to make a deal happen. Adding to this chaos was a hard deadline of closing the deal in 90 days. Mutek was slated to go public in June, so the acquisition had to close by March 31, 2000.

In the midst of this mayhem, my partners and I met and decided to give away 5 percent of the deal to our employees. But while this decision seemed innocent enough to us, it was received with what seemed like implacable opposition. The same accountants and lawyers on both sides of the deal who were fighting incessantly over the placement of a comma in the final contract were now magically unified in their opposition to our plan.

They did make some good points. First of all, restructuring the deal would take valuable time—time they insisted we did not have. If the deal did not happen by March 31, it would not happen at all. Second, giving away the cash portion of the deal was one thing, but giving stock would mean that our people would incur taxable income without the money to pay the taxes. Finally, they argued that since RGI had never created a stock plan, we had no legal obligation to put the deal in jeopardy in order to cut our employees in. In fact, they argued, didn't we have a moral obligation to our employees to make sure the deal happened? Mutek planned to create stock options for all the employees after the public offering. Why not set aside our plan for now and make it up to them down the road?

But despite the persuasiveness of their arguments, the excruciating pressure they imposed, and our own desire to see the deal happen, we held firm. And to our great relief, the deal closed on time and the employees' stock was turned into options so that no tax liability was incurred.

A year later I was in Israel for a board meeting when I bumped into one of the lead lawyers in our deal. He took me aside and reminded me that shortly after we closed the deal, the stock market collapsed, bringing the irrational exuberance of the "dot com" feeding frenzy to a crashing end. He told me that had we held up the deal for even a few weeks, it would never have gotten done, and, even if it had, my partners and I would have had to take a big reduction in valuation. When I agreed with his analysis, he said, "So I have to ask you, are your employees better, more motivated, or more loyal?"

I had to admit that after the initial euphoria wore off, I couldn't point to anything specific.

"So what did you learn?," he said, almost triumphantly.

"I learned that I'd do it again in a heartbeat."

With that he just shook his head and walked away with the air of man who had long since learned that there's just no use arguing with some people.

But, of course, we did get something out of it. We got the immense satisfaction that comes with knowing that we did the right thing. We got proof that our commitment to service and selflessness was not just a platitude to use to our advantage when things were good but to quickly abandon when the pressure was on. Our generosity was not rooted in a desire for gratefulness, loyalty, and increased productivity on the part of our employees. It was rooted in our own gratitude for services they had already rendered. And I firmly believe that if our employees had not unconsciously sensed all along that we were the kind of people who would behave in such a way, we would never have built a company worth buying in the first place.

What the lawyer who approached me didn't understand, and what I despaired of explaining to him, is that the future can cause the present just as easily as the present can cause the future. Just as with the stock market, it is what people expect to happen in the future that often determines how they invest their precious time and energy in the present.

Ethical behavior, like all the Trappist virtues, does not result from a decision but from a way of life. To consistently make ethical choices we must become ethical people who do the right thing most of the time without even thinking about it, and this cannot be accomplished by taking a class. Instead it is one of the things that taking the Hero's Journey of personal transformation from selfishness to selflessness brings about.

9

FAITH

ONE DAY I ASKED Mepkin's abbot, Father Francis, how he and his brothers managed to get so much accomplished with so few resources. He smiled and said, "We just trust the process. This is a 1,500-year-old tradition. We just trust the process."

Mepkin's success relies on faith. But this is not just the kind of faith we usually associate with a laundry list of theological beliefs. Instead it is the kind of faith that is implicit in the word *faithful*. Belief in a religious proposition, like the virginity of Mary, is a static model, but it is the dynamic model of faithfulness—faith in action—that is far more important to the business success of Mepkin Abbey. The monks' success relies on faithfully behaving in ways that may not seem entirely rational to the casual observer or even at times to the monks themselves. And if we want to share in their success, we must live the same way.

Several years ago an organization called People for the Ethical Treatment of Animals (PETA) targeted Mepkin Abbey's egg business as a way to bring media attention to what they consider the "inhumane" treatment of chickens. The PETA protest was based purely on the fact that Mepkin's well-fed and pampered chickens happened to live in cages. Despite the fact that Mepkin's standards far exceeded government regulations, the media latched onto the story and gathered at Mepkin's gates for a noisy press conference organized by PETA. Soon there were articles throughout the country echoing PETA's fanciful claim that the monks were "abusing" chickens.

But what PETA and the media failed to consider was the level of local support that Our Lady of Mepkin had among her consumers and distributors. Soon a full-blown backlash was under way, and local grocery stores even went so far as to publicly proclaim their support for Mepkin through signs in their windows and open letters posted to their Web sites. Yet despite this groundswell and clear evidence that the tide was turning, I eventually heard that Mepkin was planning to exit their egg business.

I worked intimately with Mepkin's chickens for years without ever seeing even the slightest evidence of ill treatment. I admit that when I found out that Mepkin's monks were abandoning their egg business, I was so angry that the first thing I did was call the PETA executive behind the media circus and let him know how wrong his organization was about Mepkin's chickens. The next thing I did was call Father Stan, the heart and soul of Mepkin's egg business, who had recently succeeded Father Francis as Mepkin's abbot.

Stan told me that the decision to exit the egg business was not precipitated by any business concern (egg demand was actually up), but simply because Mepkin did not want any more adverse publicity for the bakers, restaurants, grocery stores, and local government officials who had so loyally supported Mepkin for so many years. While Stan seemed grateful for my support, in the hour that we talked, he evinced no anger and never mentioned the abbey's plight at losing its main source of income. Finally I asked him how he intended to make ends meet.

"Oh, I don't know," he replied softly, with a chuckle. "We'll figure something out. Trappists always do."

Here was a man who had invested his entire life in a business, only to see the brand he had painstakingly built unfairly maligned. Yet he was treating its untimely demise almost nonchalantly, with no concern for whether his decision might be construed as an implicit admission of guilt. All he and his brothers cared about was helping others who might be adversely affected by all the publicity—even though there was no pressure from these same people to do so. What's more, he was leaving the egg business despite the fact that he had no idea just how he was going to replace the lost revenue that paid the monastery's bills. Once again I was an eyewitness to the heroic faithfulness that a life of service and selflessness requires.

After shuttering their egg business, the brothers had to start from scratch. When I suggested going into a service business, Stan demurred. He said the community was committed to the Trappist tradition of making a living through manual labor. Eventually Mepkin went into the mushroom business, raising and marketing exotic varieties. And despite their lack of experience and many rookie mistakes, the brothers faithfully persevered. Today the business is not only doing well but has the potential to be far more lucrative than producing eggs ever was. It was faith in the principles and virtues of the monastic tradition that guided the monks of Mepkin on this new journey into the unknown with their very livelihood at stake. Detachment and service to others led to the decision to leave their egg business behind, but it was faith that powered their conviction that somehow, in a way they could not imagine at the time, things would turn out for the best if they just had the courage to do "the right thing."

In today's rapidly changing and increasingly disruptive marketplace, it is these exact same virtues that are so sorely needed and so often found wanting. Most businesses today must continually "reinvent" themselves to be successful, and the annals of business are littered with once-great companies, like Kodak, that couldn't bring themselves to abandon or cannibalize their "cash cow" in the face of rapidly evolving markets. Many analysts, for example, believe that Microsoft's myopic addiction to Windows and Microsoft Office led the company to miss the opportunity presented by the Internet—a missed opportunity that, despite billions of dollars in investment, Microsoft has been unable to retrieve. Meanwhile, Steve Jobs took a leap of faith. Rather than remain a bit player in the computer business, he took Apple on a heroic journey into the unknown. This journey has transformed Apple into the most valuable company in history, built on an array of products and services that even Jobs himself could barely have imagined when he decided to "bet the company" on an unproven strategy.

In business and our personal lives, it is usually fear of the unknown that keeps us from making the changes we need to make to meet life's challenges. We need faith in something bigger than ourselves to overcome this fear and face these challenges. I recently saw the documentary *Steve Jobs: One Last Thing*, which emphasized the impact that his lifelong interest in Zen Buddhism had on his work. The documentary mainly recounted the ways in which Zen's tradition of artistic simplicity influenced Apple's products, but I think there is more to it than that. Jobs's faith involved more than a belief in his own genius. His faith also meant creating products "for the rest of us." It was his fanatical focus on delighting other people that turned Jobs into a high-tech evangelist decked out in the almost clerical collar of his black turtleneck shirt. It was a commitment to others that produced his uncanny sense for knowing exactly what his customers wanted to buy.

As I've alluded to previously, Jesus said that if we seek first the kingdom of God, everything else will take care of itself, and this is the kind of faith that drives the monks of Mepkin. The monks attack each and every day with the faith that if they "live the life" of service and selflessness, the necessities will somehow be provided.

This way of life is not limited to monasteries, Christians, or even believers. Over the years I've watched in awe as people from all over the world and from all walks of life have stepped forward to help the monks live out their mission. As with the local support they received in the face of PETA's onslaught, the brothers never ask for outside help, yet it seems to flow effortlessly. Mepkin's mood of higher purpose is so seductive that people step forward to help and go away feeling as if they got the better part of the bargain, and there is no reason why our corporate customers, vendors, and colleagues can't feel the same way.

A colleague of mine once complained that the monastic model was not applicable to business because the monks have the unfair advantage of "free labor." I countered that the more important issue is *why* monasteries get this level of commitment from people and our secular organizations do not. Mepkin's volunteer labor is not in fact "free." It is just that people feel they are being more than fairly compensated in something they value more than money.

I am not, of course, arguing that our secular organizations should operate without monetary compensation, but there is a point to be made. Many exciting and innovative companies have used an "open source" approach to invite unpaid outsiders to help make product enhancements—even to the point of writing free software—with impressive results. I currently write for Forbes.com as an unpaid contributor. I do so because writing for Forbes increases my reach and therefore my chances of making a difference in other people's lives. Wikipedia has created a huge Web presence based largely on unpaid labor. Initially our own company, RGI, couldn't afford to offer competitive wages. Yet despite the fact that the unemployment rate hovered around 1.5 percent in Research Triangle Park, North Carolina, during the boom years of the 1990s, we were able to use our mission and culture to attract the people we needed to be successful. These examples are not an argument for underpaying people. They merely illustrate how much people will sacrifice in order to feel part of something bigger than themselves.

Faith at Mepkin is not just about theology. It means faithfully living out the mission regardless of where it leads and how scary things get. But it is important to note that faithfully living the mission didn't mean that Mepkin had to stubbornly stick to eggs, no matter what. As I've noted before, the secret to Mepkin's business success is that the monks are actually not in business at all. Paradoxically, their commitment to a much higher mission than profit provides the detachment and in turn the flexibility that allows them to adjust their business model in response to changing circumstances.

By contrast many businesses fail because, lacking a mission that transcends economics, they foolishly stick to a strategy that is failing. Again, the bankruptcy of Eastman Kodak is a great example. Despite ample evidence that the market for film was rapidly going the way of the buggy whip, Kodak waited so long that in the end the company couldn't reinvent itself. Kodak considered its mission to be making film, and in this case faithfully pursuing its mission led only to myopic folly. Having a much larger mission than making film, or even taking and storing pictures, may very well have helped Kodak adapt their business model to a rapidly changing environment.

One day I asked a new monk, a comparative youngster of about fifty, why he had joined the monastery.

"I almost didn't," he replied. "I was meeting with Father Stan, and I said, 'If I join and take care of all these old men, who's going to be around to take care of me?'"

"'I don't know,' Stan replied. 'All I know for sure is that I'll be here.' I was so moved by his answer that I signed up on the spot."

Father Stan's conviction and this new monk's reaction is the kind of faith that Mepkin is built on, and it is critical to Mepkin's business success. And in my own business experience I have seen just how powerful this faith can be.

AS I MENTIONED PREVIOUSLY, after scrambling for a few months, our company, RGI, became a reseller of a developer's tool called SourceSafe. As a version-control package, SourceSafe had a distinct advantage over other tools: it was designed to be used by teams of programmers. Therefore, an initial sale of a single copy inevitably led to more sales and higher dollars as teams of programmers standardized on SourceSafe.

Elated by our success with SourceSafe, we began looking around for other software tools that shared this "groupware," or team, attribute and found one in what is called "bug tracking." As its name suggests, "bug" tracking tools help teams of software developers manage the legions of bugs that inevitably crop up in their software. As with SourceSafe, bug tracking required each programmer to have his own copy, which led to bigger sales. So we began reselling Defect Control System (DCS) from a Denver company called the Software Edge. As with SourceSafe, we kept 40 percent of the selling price for each copy we sold.

We were now selling two products, and as sales slowly but steadily increased, we religiously plowed our 40 percent margins into more sales reps and lead generation. After 18 months of living a high-wire act, our business finally seemed to be taking off. Though we were still not drawing a paycheck, I was so sure that the skies were finally clearing that I wearily said to one of my partners, "Dave, I think we just may have a business."

A few days later, the bottom fell out of the tub. The chief marketing officer for the Software Edge, our bug-tracking client, called to say that the company had just been sold to a much larger firm with its own sales force. As soon as the deal closed, RGI's services would no longer be needed. Our investment in their product, DCS, would become a total loss. The news was devastating, especially when the CMO told me by way of thanks that the spike in sales that RGI had produced for DCS had been instrumental in turning the Software Edge into an acquisition target.

Then, a week later, Kenny Felder called. One Tree Software, the manufacturer of SourceSafe, was in the process of being sold to Microsoft. Again, once the deal went through, RGI's services would no longer be needed.

This blow, hard on the heels of the news from the Software Edge, took me to my knees. All the work, sacrifice, and strain, and we were right back where we started. The only thing that had changed is that we now had a higher payroll to meet every two weeks.

I had never felt so utterly defeated, and after conveying the news that Microsoft was buying SourceSafe to my partners, I announced that I had had enough. I told them that they could either soldier on without me or we could wind the company down. Though my partners were clearly devastated, no one tried to dissuade me from my decision. It was a Friday, and after they dejectedly filed out of my office, I went home early—the first time I had done so since we started RGI.

Then, for the entire weekend, I sleeplessly wrestled with myself. On the one hand, all the typical reasons for sticking it out no longer held any weight. I didn't care about being a CEO and entrepreneur or the wealth that this might bring. Financially, I still had some money in the bank, and I knew that with my skill set and résumé, I would never starve. Even the prospect of admitting defeat held no terrors. I'd had plenty of success in the past, I reasoned, and better men than I had been defeated and recovered. Hell, some of them even considered their defeats more valuable than their victories. Besides, maybe the humility I would get from defeat would do me some good.

The longer I thought about it, the longer the list of reasons why I should quit lengthened. By contrast, on the other side of the ledger, there was only one reason to reverse my decision and stick it out instead. My first teacher—the wild, wonderful Zen master Richard Rose—had drilled into my head the importance of commitment. And the most important commitment of all was keeping your word to your friends, no matter what. Rose's exalted sense of loyalty had, in turn, become a cornerstone in my own philosophy: a principle that I never tired of espousing to the students of the SKS and our adult group.

Throughout the weekend my mind kept returning to the fact that by quitting, I was turning my back on my friends. My partners didn't want to quit, but I knew that without me, they would be forced to close the business. No amount of rationalization could relieve me from the awful truth that I was betraying my friends and community. I knew in my heart that I had to find the faith to practice what I preached.

So early Monday morning, I again met with my partners. "Listen," I said. "I have no idea how we are going to survive. But I do know this. I'm not quitting. If you guys want to stick it out, I'm in it with you. The only way I'm leaving this company is on a stretcher, feet first."

For the next few months, we lived on the brink of disaster. The deal for the Software Edge closed, and our bug-tracking revenue disappeared, but we heard absolutely nothing from One Tree. So we continued to sell SourceSafe while I desperately and unsuccessfully searched for other products to sell. All we could do was faithfully continue to give our best as we waited for word from One Tree.

Our persistence paid off. After a multimonth delay, One Tree was finally acquired, but rather than send RGI packing, as we had feared, Microsoft made RGI the sole provider of the current version of SourceSafe while their own programmers gave it the look and feel of a Microsoft product. The Microsoft acquisition electrified the market. Suddenly every programmer wanted SourceSafe, and RGI was the only place in the world to get it. It was as if the heavens had magically opened over RGI and rained down money by the bucket.

Better yet, during this transition we forged a relationship with Microsoft that led to RGI building its own bug-tracking product, Visual Intercept, to complement the newly renamed Microsoft

Visual SourceSafe. The acquisition of SourceSafe transformed RGI from a software reseller to a manufacturer, and, with Microsoft's marketing muscle behind us, Visual Intercept rapidly became the number-one bug-tracking tool on the market. This, in turn, eventually led to the acquisition of our company. Rather than the disaster I had feared, One Tree's acquisition by Microsoft turned out to be the best thing that could have happened to RGI.

○

THE RGI STORY would have had a radically different ending if I had followed through on my intention to quit RGI in the face of adversity and an unknown future. In retrospect this story can easily be mapped onto the Hero's Journey.

The Call represents our desire to start a company, and the Resistance to the Call, our initial hesitancy to do so. The Desert is represented by all the agony we went through for two years as we fought desperately against long odds to build a sustainable business. The Great Trial happened when, just as we were finally beginning to relax, everything seemed to fall apart. Death and Rebirth is captured neatly by how close we came to killing our company, and the way our decision to go on without hope led to a magical outcome we could never have predicted. Death and Rebirth is also a great way to describe how RGI's business model was utterly transformed by the One Tree acquisition. And the Return to Help Others maps to building a relationship with Microsoft, expanding our ability to help customers by creating a new product, selling the company, and making sure that everyone shared in the proceeds.

But taking the Hero's Journey in the first place relies on faith, and faith relies on community. One day, while we were still deep in the Desert, my brother Tom came into my office. He told me that he had spent every dime he had working without pay for RGI. He literally didn't have enough money to eat. Yet the only thing I saw on his face was the agony of a man whose only concern was the thought that he was letting his friends down. I managed to get him to accept some money from me to tide him over, but I later got a much bigger gift from Tom in return. When things seemed to be falling apart, it was, especially, Tom's example that convinced me to stick with the company.

During that long weekend of soul searching after announcing that I was going to quit, it was the picture of my brother Tom, playing his role as the faithful and impoverished monk, that kept coming back to me again and again. It was his example of faithfulness and the faithfulness of my other partners that led to my decision to go on—a decision that I would never have made for myself.

When I look back, I see more than a Great Trial for RGI. My own faith was tested in the Desert, and I came dangerously close to losing the Promised Land, not only for myself but for all the people I cared about most. In the end what saved me was not just my faith in myself or my principles. It was the faith I borrowed from others.

God does indeed work in mysterious ways, but like the monks of Mepkin Abbey, we must have the faith to meet him halfway, no matter how scary it gets.

10

THE POWER OF TRUST

THE PROBLEM WITH LIFE is that it must be lived forward and only understood backward. My journey to Mepkin Abbey started with an accident: an event that only with the benefit of 20/20 hindsight became what I now consider the happiest accident of my life.

During the winter of 1996, the Duke SKS students decided to go skydiving as a team-building exercise and begged me to go along. As soon as I reluctantly agreed, I was struck for the first time in my life with a profound sense of foreboding. I ignored it—apparently I had enough courage to jump out of an airplane, but not enough to tell a bunch of college kids that I was too damn old to be jumping out of airplanes.

The free fall with an expert "tandem jumper" strapped to my back was uneventful. The parachute opened on cue, and the next thing I knew the ground was slowly rising to meet me. But as I touched down, I watched in amazement as my right foot turned completely around in its socket; something I didn't know that it could do. I crumpled to the ground in agony roundly cursing skydiving and skydivers until the ambulance arrived.

As they rushed me into surgery at the hospital, I plaintively asked one of the nurses whether I was going to be all right. "You're awake, that's a helluva lot more than I can say for most of the damn fools they bring in here from that place," she snapped, with the air of someone firmly convinced that I needed a psychiatrist far more than a surgeon.

When I awoke from surgery I learned that I had compound fractured my ankle. "You drove one hell of a lot of energy through that ankle," the surgeon said. "We used 13 pins and in some places the bone was so crushed that all we could do was press the little pieces back in place like a mosaic."

I spent a week in the hospital hooked to a morphine drip. I was also hit by wave after wave of panic attacks which I could not understand. My injury was not *that* serious. Finally, it hit me. My broken ankle was only the catalyst. For the first time in my life I was facing my own mortality. Yes, this time I would recover, but the day would soon arrive when no amount of doctoring would save me, and this realization produced waves of fresh panic.

I felt utterly isolated as the hospital staff bustled around me, apparently oblivious to the fact that death was waiting patiently for them as well. I wanted to grab them by the lapels and shake them out of their complacency. Instead I said nothing and was racked by guilt for wanting to replace their chirpy cheerfulness with my own emotional agony.

Worst of all, despite all the years I'd spent forging a "spiritual path," I realized that I was utterly unprepared for death. The chips were down, and the only thing I cared about was what the doctors could do for me. When I was released from the hospital the panic attacks gradually subsided only to be replaced with the profound feeling that I had been irrevocably damaged. I felt hollowed out inside and the world had turned gray and lifeless. Returning to work at RGI, I just couldn't recover the energy and enthusiasm I'd had before the accident, and I felt guilty for making my partners pick up the slack.

Desperate to regain my footing, I hit the gym hard, hoping to accelerate my rehab and shake off these growing feelings of despair. One day I was maniacally working the Step Climber when I heard a voice.

"Not feeling too good, are you, Aug?"

Swiveling my head I saw a casual gym acquaintance named Hugh. With his parted hair hanging past his shoulders and a full mustache, he looked like an in-shape, blue-collar version of the rock star David Crosby. Startled by his sudden appearance and the nature of his comment, my first inclination was to brush him off with a lie. But there was something about the quiet compassion in his glittering brown eyes that compelled the truth. So I nodded instead.

"Yeah," he said in a soft southern drawl, "in AA we call it the soul hole. Feels like your heart's broken, don't it?" I was amazed— that was exactly how I felt, though I'd never put it that way before. I nodded again.

"Listen, I'm here to tell you that you're in for two years of so much hell you'll be wishin' you was never born. But you'll get through it and come out the other side. And when you do, you're gonna like yourself a whole lot more than you do right now. The only thing that'll be left is gratitude. Pure gratitude." His prophecy complete, Hugh turned and walked away and I never saw him again.

One week later I got a phone call from Josh Skudlarick, a Duke SKS student who had just graduated.

"Augie," Josh said, "I just wanted you to know that at least one of your students is taking you up on your advice."

"What advice?"

"You told us to do something with our summer vacation besides drinking beer and getting a tan. I'm spending the summer as a monastic guest at a Trappist monastery called Mepkin Abbey."

While I couldn't remember proffering the advice, I was thrilled for Josh and plied him with questions about his monastic routine.

But as he patiently fielded my fusillade of questions, what really struck me was the change I sensed in him. I'd known Josh for several years, and in two short months as a Trappist he seemed to have been transformed from an angst-ridden boy into a quietly confident young man.

Suddenly I knew what I needed to do. "I want to come," I said, interrupting Josh mid-sentence.

"When?" he replied, obviously taken aback by the urgency in my voice.

"Right now," I said, then hastily corrected myself. "I mean, this weekend."

"I'll ask Brother John," Josh said. A few minutes later he returned with an invitation for a weekend retreat at Mepkin. Josh must have made quite an impression on the monks—the waiting list for Mepkin retreats, especially over weekends, usually stretches out for months.

I arrived Friday afternoon, and after checking into one of the guesthouses sprinkled around the grounds for retreatants, I headed to the church for Vespers. At the stroke of six, the bells pealed. The monks stood up, bowed to the altar, and a voice sang out, "Oh God, come to my assistance!" The community took up the refrain, "Lord make haste to help me!" It was my first service at Mepkin, and these words made me think of Hugh's prophecy. If the hell he had foretold—and that resonated so strongly with my own sense of dread—was going to be anything like the hell I'd just gone through with my ankle, I wanted all God's help I could get.

I was so impressed by the monks that I returned to Mepkin several times in quick succession. When Christmas rolled around, I wrote to Brother John asking to come for several weeks as a monastic guest, and was accepted. One day during my Christmas stay I asked the abbot, Dom Francis, if I could speak to him privately. He agreed and I told him about the way I had been feeling since my accident. He listened intently and sympathetically, and told me that he had noticed that I'd been volunteering for extra work around the monastery and he urged me to continue to do so. Then he told me that he had already asked Father Christian, Mepkin's 82-year-old former abbot, to meet with me as well—a man who would end up being my spiritual director as well as one of the kindest, wisest, most trustworthy men I would ever know. At his office door, as the visit ended, Dom Francis gave me a hug and told me something that has guided me ever since, whether I am actually visiting Mepkin or not: "Augie, the monastic tradition is a 1,500-year-old process. Trust that process."

SOONER OR LATER every executive realizes that 99 percent of the people she depends on for success don't report to her. The success of every CEO depends far more on vendors, stockholders, board members, regulators, politicians, strategic partners, the financial community, the media, and customers than it does on the relatively small number of paid employees that report to her either directly or indirectly. I was very successful in sales at MTV, but my success relied far more on the help and support I got from the legal, finance, marketing, research, and engineering folks than it did on my own people or my own skills. Real leadership is built on persuasion, and persuasion relies on trust. Louis R. Mobley, my mentor and the director of the IBM Executive School, said that business relies on the trusting process he called "promise and fulfillment." Few people realize that the all-important corporate profit-and-loss statement (P&L) contains no cash or real money. It consists primarily of accounts receivable and accounts payable, which in turn are merely the promises that others make to pay us and the promises we make to pay others at some future date. Without the trust that underlies these promises commerce would grind to a halt.

Even cash depends on trust. We accept intrinsically worthless pieces of paper and plastic cards in exchange for goods and services because we trust that others will do the same. The United States income tax is primarily a voluntary system. The IRS largely trusts us to pay our taxes, while in many other countries the mistrust that underlies tax evasion and corruption cripples their economic and civic life. On a trip I took to St. Petersburg, a Russian woman crisply summed up a thousand years of Russian misery in a single sentence. "There is no trust in Russia." Every contract relies on trust, and when marketing gurus endlessly praise "authentic brands" they are merely describing brands that consumers can trust. Unless we could trust other drivers to stay on their side of the road, driving would be impossible, and Canada and the United States share the benefits of the longest unguarded border in the world because of mutual trust.

The surest way to amass the power you need to effectively manage your life is to use the Hero's Journey to *become* the kind of person that others instinctively trust—especially when something critical is at stake. A trustworthy person is not self-interested or uninterested. He is *disinterested* and *detached,* and the more disinterested you become the more powerful you will be. Father Christian and Father Francis were not born trustworthy, nor did it happen overnight. They *became* people I could entrust with my life by dedicating their own lives to the Hero's Journey of personal transformation. I now refer to the two years that followed my skydiving accident as the Great Trial on my own Hero's Journey. The hell that Hugh predicted came to pass with a vengeance, but Father Christian, Father Francis, and the monks of Mepkin were there for me every step of the way. And just like Hugh also prophesized, all that now remains is gratitude. Pure gratitude.

◯

I WAS ONCE BROUGHT in to turn around sales for a large company. The company was rapidly losing money, and this had led to the most vicious interdepartmental infighting I've ever seen. The various executives were not even speaking to each other, let alone cooperating. Everyone in my department, from directors to assistants, expected me to take up cudgels and defend the sales department, and I spent my first day on the job meeting privately with all the people lined up at my door, determined to make sure that I had a complete list of all their grievances.

I listened intently to each one and took copious notes. When they finished venting I said the same thing to each one.

"That's terrible. How long has this situation been going on?"

"Over a year," was more or less the universal reply.

"Wow, that long? Well, if you've been putting up with it for a year I know I can count on you to hang in there for a few more days while I come up with my plan."

Having bought some time, I closed the door and did some hard thinking. I had to do something fast, but what? I felt overwhelmed until I asked myself what a *service and selflessness* response to my predicament might be. Then I picked up the phone and asked each of the other department heads for an appointment, carefully making it clear that the meeting would take place in their offices, on their turf.

When I arrived with my pencil and legal pad, I was universally greeted by an executive with folded arms and barely concealed hostility, barricaded snugly behind his desk. Taking a seat, I leaned forward and gently said, "I'm here to find out what sales can do to make your life easier."

It took a while for the shock to fade from their faces, but eventually they were rattling off their suggestions as I scribbled them down. Their grievances were legitimate, and as I wrote them down I marveled that none of my own people seemed to be aware of them.

One high crime and misdemeanor perpetrated by sales I'll never forget. Each of the company's customer support reps had two telephone lines. One was for in-bound customer calls and the other was for internal use only. If a customer called in for support and was put on hold, he would call his salesman. The sales rep would then transfer his customer to a support rep's private line and instantly hang up. Thinking the call was coming from his supervisor, the support rep would pick up, only to be saddled with two irate customers—one for each ear.

After taking inventory with the other executives, I gathered my department together and told them that my immediate priority was convincing everyone in the company that our only interest was in serving the overall mission. I told them that we would have to earn the trust of the other departments by getting our own house in order first. This, of course, was not what they wanted to hear, and for a few moments everyone just sat there shell-shocked. I then made a personal appeal for their trust, and they agreed to go along. (My plea was bolstered by sharing with them the sordid fruits of my investigation. When I brought up what I later learned the sales reps referred to as "dropping calls" on support reps, the news was greeted by doe-eyed shock—how had such a nefarious thing been going on right under their collective noses! But hell, at least no one denied it.)

It took a few weeks, but when the other departments saw that I was following through on my promises and asking for nothing in return, one by one they stopped by and offered to reciprocate. Little by little mutual trust was established, and I went from feeling powerless to feeling as if I had more than enough influence to accomplish my goals. Four months later sales had taken off, the company was profitable, and we were all socializing together. Sales threw the first inter-departmental party and it took the better part of an hour and a keg of beer before the first brave souls ventured from their departmental enclaves at the corners of the room, crossed no-man's-land, and mingled with their former enemies. An hour later, aided by a second keg, we were all fast friends.

Did I know going in that things would work out the way they did? No, I was scared to death. But as Father Francis said, I knew I had to trust the process. This experience taught me what it means to be what I later came to call a Corporate Statesman. A Corporate Statesman is an impartial, honest broker who puts the interest of the whole before his selfish interests and trusts others to follow his lead.

Trust is the most powerful tool that a leader or organization can have, and that trust is directly proportional to selflessness. If I had been trying to game my colleagues, they would have seen through it immediately, with disastrous results. Everything hinged on my willingness to subsume my selfish interests and sincerely put the company's mission and the interests of others first.

Trust is critical to monastic business success as well. The same trust I found in the offices of Father Christian and Father Francis shows up in everything even remotely connected to Mepkin. One day I was stopped for speeding at a notorious speed trap about 100 miles from Mepkin. I told the judge that I had not been speeding, and when he found out I was on my way to Mepkin he said, "Well, if you're going to Mepkin and you say you weren't speeding then you weren't speeding." He dismissed the case.

Our Lady of Mepkin's customers trust her products. Mepkin's suppliers trust their invoices. Mepkin's volunteers and donors know they are contributing to a good cause, and Mepkin's reservoir of trust spilled over into my speeding ticket 100 miles from the monastery.

Trust is the most powerful form of capital there is, and nothing makes a business run more smoothly than trust. In addition, trust is not a scarce resource. Like Mepkin, we can all have more of it than we need. Warren Buffett has spent his life accumulating trust, and this trust is directly responsible for the "Buffett Discount" he often gets when he buys a company. Sellers know that he will treat them honorably, and this is so valuable that they are willing to accept Buffett's offer even when richer offers are on the table. However, while trust is not a scarce resource, it is a fragile asset. Once squandered it may be impossible to regain.

◯

A CLOSE EXAMINATION of the case study above and my Mepkin experience holds some valuable lessons on how to get and maintain trust.

1. *Become Trustworthy.* We are hardwired to seek out trustworthy people, and to test others to see whom we can trust. But the first step is to become trustworthy ourselves. Like attracts like, and if you invest in becoming a person others can trust people whom you can trust will be attracted to you.

2. *Keep Your Promises.* The surest mark of a trustworthy person is one who keeps his promises. Keep small or even trivial promises because others will gauge your reliability on the big things from how you handle the little ones, even if they are not consciously aware of it. Lou Mobley, for example, was highly suspicious of people who couldn't be on time. While it was never a deal breaker, anyone habitually late was starting in a hole with Mobley.

3. *Keep Promises to Yourself.* It is an unfortunate human failing that we insist on virtues in others that we don't develop in ourselves. Keeping promises to yourself is closely correlated with willpower and self-control, and these virtues are essential to being trustworthy—especially when the chips are down. Remember, willpower is like any other muscle. No matter how out of shape your willpower may be, if you engage in daily exercises like being on time you will gradually master yourself.

4. *Under Commit and Over Deliver.* Make sure that you only make promises that you know you can keep. We overcommit because we want people to love and respect us, yet the quickest way to lose love and respect is to fail to keep our promises. Get in the habit of writing down every promise you make, no matter how trivial. This will give you a way to manage your promise making and evaluate how well you are doing in keeping them.

5. *Be Willing to Make Promises.* One of the stratagems that notoriously unreliable people use is refusing to make promises in

the first place. This fallacious line of reasoning argues that if you don't make any promises, you don't have to worry about breaking them. People quickly see through this strategy, and even more quickly you will get the reputation not only for unreliability but for being indecisive as well. Remember that a refusal to make a decision is just another kind of decision.

6. *Protect Your Personal Brand.* We usually think of a brand as something that belongs to laundry soap. But we all have a personal brand. Like a good brand manager, get in the habit of constantly asking yourself, "How will this decision affect my personal brand?" P&G keeps an army of lawyers on retainer just to make sure that Tide is not associated with the "wrong" kinds of people, places, and things. Similarly, AA insists that the recovering alcoholic concentrate on replacing the people, places, and things that he associates with drinking with more positive influences. Everything you do or don't do affects your brand, and in the long run your reputation is your most valuable asset.

7. *Eradicate Ambiguity.* Nothing undermines trust faster than ambiguity. We default to phrases like "I'll try" in order to furnish plausible deniability when we fail to deliver. Many of the "he said, she said" controversies that produce so much friction in business are caused by ambiguous attempts by everyone involved to stay off the hook. Almost every time I run down one of these disagreements I find that the real culprit is a failure by the parties involved to be clear and specific in the first place about who is promising what to whom by when.

8. *Institutionalize Promise Keeping.* At our own company, RGI, we institutionalized promise keeping. Every critical task had to have its own paper trail that included a clear understanding of who was involved, the promise made, and the criteria by which the promise could be determined as fulfilled. My partners and I relentlessly managed this process, and the little bit of extra effort up front that it took to produce this paper trail paid off handsomely in time saved and ill will avoided after the fact.

9. *Never Make People Ask.* If you make people hound you about a promise, you have already lost half of your credibility. If one of your people is up for review and must ask you for it, you usually end up giving a bigger raise while receiving little goodwill in return. Nothing builds trust better than anticipating your obligations and delivering on them without being asked. A debt repaid before it is asked for reaps a huge dividend in trust. The money that changes hands is the same, but the trust equation is radically different.

10. *Communicate, Communicate, Communicate.* No one can keep all their promises, but there is no excuse for a failure to communicate that we may be unable to deliver. We often avoid communicating from embarrassment or the fear of admitting failure, but this only leads others to assume that you had no intention of keeping your promise and were hoping that they would fail to notice. Get in the habit of preemptively sending status reports on your promises. If everything is going to plan you spare others from worrying, and if not you give them time to go to Plan B.

11. *Aim Past the Target.* It is impossible to be trustworthy in business if you are unreliable in the rest of your life. The monks of Mepkin give little thought to that narrow field called "business ethics." Like my speeding ticket, the trust that the monks enjoy in business merely spills over from the way they live their lives. Trust for the monks is not a business strategy or tactic; it is the natural by-product of living for a higher purpose. Conversely, if you value trust for its selfish utility value alone, you will most likely fail in your efforts.

Trust begins with the kind of faith we discussed in the last chapter. Faith provides the courage to go first, before we are sure about the way things will turn out. Faith offers our own trust before we are sure that it will be reciprocated. This is the scary part of authentic trust, and it is authentic trust that Mepkin offers every day. There are no locks at Mepkin, and yes, once in a while things are stolen, but in the long run the trusting attitude symbolized by this lock-free environment has paid Mepkin back hundreds of times over. At RGI we concentrated on building this same kind of trusting relationship with our customers, and though we never ran a credit check, we collected virtually every nickel of millions of dollars in receivables without ever suing a single customer.

11

SELF-KNOWLEDGE AND
AUTHENTICITY

The stresses of high-altitude mountain climbing reveal
your true character; they unmask who you really are.
You no longer have the social graces to hide behind, to
play roles. You are the essence of what you are.
—*David Breashears*

TO THIS DAY I know virtually nothing about Brother William. I don't know where he was born, how he was raised, or when and why he decided to become a Trappist monk. And since he passed away a few years ago, it is unlikely I'll learn much more. Yet Brother William and I were very close, and this ability to become very close to someone you know nothing about is something I've only experienced at Mepkin.

Brother William was a warm and affable monk, slightly stooped with a full head of closely cropped gray hair and a singing voice worthy of the schola (monastic choir). He and Brother Edward, the monastery's chef, lived next door to each other in the cloister and were the best of friends. On his way to his choir stall for monastic services, Brother Edward would often stop at Brother William's stall to rub him playfully on the head, and it gave me a warm feeling to occasionally see them softly chatting tête-à-tête in the breezeway outside their rooms, even though, strictly speaking, speaking behind the cloister wall was strictly forbidden. In the spirit that every rule is made to be broken, these forbidden confabulations between intimate friends seemed more laudable than forgivable, and I can only surmise that the abbot and their brothers felt the same way.

I can't recall just how Brother William and I got so close. William was responsible for the button in the refectory that sounds the chimes throughout the monastery calling the brothers to prayer and meals, and perhaps it was my playful request to push "the magic button"—a request to which he readily acceded—that first broke the ice. However our friendship started, by the summer of 1997, William and I were as thick as thieves. I was at the midpoint of what I described in the previous chapter as my Great Trial, and things had gotten so bad that I took a leave of absence from my company in order to spend the entire summer at Mepkin. Continuing to follow Father Francis's advice about extra work, I volunteered for kitchen duty and mowing grass, besides my steady job packing eggs. In lieu of my one-hour siesta after the midday meal, I would grab my push mower and cut grass until it was time for the afternoon shift at the egg house. After work I would mow like a maniac until it was time to set out the cheese, salad, and fruit that make up the light fare of the optional monastic meal of supper. After supper I would finish cleaning up just in time to make it to Vespers at six. I even got permission from Dom Francis to cut grass all day Sunday, as long as I stayed far enough away from the monastery proper that my mower didn't disturb the community.

The South Carolina sun often sent the thermometer well north of 100 degrees, and I would occasionally take a break from mowing and head to the monastery for some water or juice. There, liberally plastered with sweat, dirt, and grass clippings, I would often run into Brother William, who always took an inordinate delight in seeing me in such a splendid condition. "Wild Man!" he would exclaim with a grin, and no matter how dirty and sweaty I was, we would exchange a bear hug, with me hoisting his smaller frame several inches off the ground. "Wow, I wish I could work like that," he once lamented after our embrace, a comment that gained added significance when I later learned that he was already suffering from the chronic lung disease that eventually killed him.

One afternoon I was shoving my mower in the scorching heat near the circle where the roads leading to the monastery proper, the Luce Gardens, and the monastery farm come together. Looking up, I saw Brother William arriving from the refectory with some water. After my drink, William and I settled into the oak-shaded park bench near the statue of the Sacred Heart that guards the traffic circle.

Brother William confided that back in the 1960s, he had lived for several years as a hermit in the thick woods surrounding the monastery grounds. I had visited some of these simple shelters, or "hermitages," which the monks had erected over the years as refuges for solitary prayer, and I immediately began bombarding William with questions about his life as a hermit. As Brother William patiently fielded my questions, I discovered that he, like many other Trappists, had been inspired to solitary prayer by the example of Thomas Merton, the famous writer, mystic, and monk who had become a hermit at the Trappist monastery of Gethsemani in Kentucky.

As I asked more and more questions, I kept the question I really wanted to ask in check, fearing that it was too personal. But curiosity finally got the best of me, and I asked, "Brother William, did you get anything out of it?"

Brother William was leaning on his knees with his eyes focused on the ground, and for what seemed like a very long time, he said nothing. Then, just as I was thinking I'd gone too far, his head slowly turned.

"I had to face myself," he said softly, and resumed his previous position.

I was left speechless by his powerful admission. I had underestimated the depth and breadth of this simple man, and I was deeply flattered that he trusted me to understand the magnitude of his achievement without further elaboration. Brother William and I sat silently under that oak tree for another 20 minutes or so, and I've never felt closer or more grateful to another human being in my life.

Several years later, even his wheelchair and the supplemental oxygen it carried were no longer enough. Brother William took to a bed in the infirmary, where I visited him one last time. A few days later, he asked for a steak and a bottle of beer, which Eddie happily provided, and a few hours after that, Brother William drifted into eternity, at peace with his God, his brothers, and, perhaps most importantly, himself.

I'VE SPENT MY LIFE searching for the "deep structures" that knit all religious traditions together, and every tradition considers self-knowledge an essential aspect of a spiritual path. My patron saint, St. Augustine, is often described as the father of psychology because of his obsessive fascination with the workings of his own heart. A visitor who sought advice from the Oracle of Delphi was reportedly greeted with an inscription: "Know Yourself and You Will Know the Gods and Heavens as Well." The same oracle considered Socrates the wisest of all men because only he knew himself well enough to realize just how ignorant he really was. Socrates, in turn, gave pride of place to self-knowledge, admonishing that the unexamined life is not worth living. The great Christian mystic Meister Eckhart said that "the eye by which I see God is the same eye by which he sees me," and Eastern traditions such as Hinduism and Buddhism teach that the way to truth is through self-knowledge. The list goes on and on, and it was this universal call to self-knowledge that led the college students I mentored to call their student organization the Self Knowledge Symposium.

Thomas Merton wrote extensively about self-knowledge, and the monastic disciplines of contemplation, sacred reading, and self-recollection are largely designed to produce just that. Yet getting to know yourself is often a painstaking and scary process, as I saw firsthand when I met a new monk who had recently traded an executive position with an Ivy League school for the white habit, or "whites," of a novice. Extending my hand I introduced myself and said, "So, Jim, how's it going so far?"

"It's hard," he said without hesitation, "harder than I ever expected and in ways I never expected."

"For instance?" I asked, taken aback by his candor.

"I'm right *here* all the time," he said, holding the palm of his hand in front of his nose like a mirror. "There's no place to run, no place to hide, just me and my demons. I thought I was leaving them behind," he finished with a gentle smile, "but I guess they just tagged along."

A *New York Times* article on Mepkin that contained interviews with a number of retreatants reinforced this point. Most spoke of the peace and tranquility, but one man added, "Yeah, it's peaceful all right. But when you sit for hours on end on a bluff overlooking the Cooper River, you end up thinking about a helluva' lot of things in your life you might rather not think about."

This experience is not restricted to monks or retreatants. I once gave a class of Duke SKS students what I thought was an easy homework assignment. For five out of the next seven days, until our next class, I asked them to stop by the Duke Chapel and sit for five minutes. They didn't have to pray or meditate—just sit. Yet week after week, these highly motivated students couldn't accomplish this simple exercise. Finally one of the boys exclaimed, "I don't get it! I pass that damn chapel a thousand times a day. Why can't I go in and sit for five minutes?"

"I don't know about you," one of the girls quietly answered, "but I know why I can't."

All eyes turned to her, and she said, "I'm terrified that I might realize that I'm wasting my life."

I can relate. The Hero's Journey might easily be described as a journey into self-knowledge, and this journey is perhaps best captured by the English word *disillusionment*. Despite our protestations to the contrary, deep down most of us fear that if we were stripped of all our "illusions," we would find ourselves—as I did when I tumbled from the heavens and into the hospital—with nothing left to fall back on. We fear that if we ever did face our demons, all we would find for our trouble is . . . well . . . demons. Or, even worse, nothing at all. Of course, according to the saints and sages of every religious tradition, what we find instead is the Death and Rebirth of the Hero's Journey. When Joseph Campbell cross-culturally researched the Hero's Journey, he found this motif endlessly repeated. Facing the pitiless dragon, as the hero must, is always just a metaphor for facing himself.

$$\bigcirc$$

IN 1955 IBM'S LEGENDARY CEO Tom Watson Jr. gave my mentor, Louis R. Mobley, and his colleagues a blank check and carte blanche to create the IBM Executive School. Fresh from successfully implementing IBM's first supervisor and middle-management training programs, Mobley confidently set about churning out executives as well.

The first thing he did, in conjunction with GE and DuPont, was hire the Educational Testing Service (ETS), the same company that still does the SATs, to identify the skills that make great leaders great. Once these intellectual skills were identified, Mobley and his colleagues at GE and DuPont assumed that spitting out executives would simply mean "training to the test."

So ETS dutifully rounded up a bunch of proven leaders and tested them extensively, looking for their common skills. The results were astounding, and more than a little disturbing. As Mobley put it, "No matter what bell-shaped curve we drew, successful leaders fell on the extreme edges. The only thing they seemed to have in common was having nothing in common. ETS was so frustrated that they offered us our money back."

But failure wasn't an option for Mobley, and he finally hit upon the answer. Unlike supervisors and middle managers, what great executives shared were not skills and knowledge, but values and attitudes. Over time Mobley identified many values that great leaders share. He discovered, for example, that great leaders thrive on ambiguity and surround themselves with the best people they can find. They crave challenges, work best under pressure, are deep thinkers, and welcome accountability.

Eventually Mobley's list became quite extensive, but he was able to subsume all the values that great leaders share under a term that monks cherish: *authenticity*. Great leaders are authentic people, and their authenticity, Mobley realized, was a by-product of self-knowledge. The reason why Brother William's admission had such a profound impact on me was because it was so authentic, and for the next 20 minutes, I'd have followed him into hell if he'd been so inclined to lead me there.

In a previous chapter, I argued that great leaders question assumptions and disrupt complacency by relentlessly asking the question: "What is the business of the business?" This exercise develops and refines organizational mission and purpose, but it is little more than the perennial "Who am I?" applied collectively in the form of "Who are we?" Mobley realized that if his students didn't know who they were and what they stood for, they could never provide those critical answers organizationally for others.

Eventually Mobley introduced me to the discipline of Organizational Development (OD), and again I was struck by the debt that OD owes to self-knowledge. OD is just organizational psychotherapy: a facilitator or coach tries to help people face their fearful "demons," the demons that produce the dysfunctional behaviors that in turn lead to dysfunctional organizations. As I discussed in the last chapter, mutual trust is the single most important asset any organization can have, and if you want to become a trustworthy person, you must first be able to trust yourself.

Once Mobley compiled his list of leadership values, he was faced with another, even more difficult problem: How do you instill values and transform attitudes? That is, how do you teach authenticity? The challenge became more formidable when he discovered that, unlike supervisors and middle managers, executives shared another trait: they were constitutionally untrainable. Worse, Mobley discovered that not only are values and attitudes impervious to typical training techniques, but hectoring people to change often had the unintended consequence of hardening existing attitudes instead.

Mobley eventually realized that authenticity required "a revolution in consciousness" rather than a step-by-step learning process. Rather than converging on a superset of skills, the IBM Executive School had to foster personal authenticity. Taking a leap of faith, he decided that what he was looking for could only be brought about as a side benefit or unintended consequence of what the monks would refer to as "spiritual work"—what we are calling the Hero's Journey.

The risk of failure was real, but if Mobley was going to produce people willing to stick out their necks, he had to stick out his own first. He abandoned lectures and books in favor of games, simulations, and experiential exercises designed not to "train," but to "blow people's minds." According to Mobley, the self-knowledge that produces authenticity does not emerge from words and abstract concepts, and while valuable, intellectual introspection, or "navel gazing," only goes so far. Self-knowledge instead is best achieved through encountering ourselves in real-life situations. These encounters don't produce incremental learning. Instead they are marked by the "all at once" insights that the monks describe as "epiphanies," "revelations," or "realizations." So Mobley's exercises were designed to produce "aha!" moments of self-realization. And most of these exercises meant attaching Brother Jim's mirror firmly to the end of the noses of IBM's executives, forcing them to face themselves and their "demons."

One exercise Mobley devised for IBM executives consisted of this case study: Bill had been a faithful and productive IBM employee for twenty years, but his performance had fallen off dramatically, and all efforts at intervention had failed. Should IBM stick with Bill or let him go?

Below the case study was a profit-and-loss statement. Along with the case study, one half of the group received a P&L that showed IBM making lots of money. The other half received a P&L that showed IBM losing lots of money. Without informing the participants of his ruse, Mobley then opened the class for discussion.

Inevitably, those who thought IBM was making money argued for keeping Bill. Those who thought IBM was running at a loss were for canning him. Yet money never came up. The competing arguments were always based on morality. Those for keeping Bill cited his long service and loyalty, while those for letting him go insisted that it was unfair to his team to keep an underperformer.

Eventually the argument would get so heated that someone would shout, "We have to let him go, we're losing money!" Followed by someone else: "What do you mean? We're making money hand over fist!"

Papers would be exchanged, the truth revealed, and a stunned silence would ensue. It was now incontrovertible that all their moralizing had been nothing but double-talk and hot air. What they had really been talking about all along was money, and, as Brother Jim had discovered in very different circumstances, there was no longer any place to hide from this truth. After this revelation, the chastened executives would usually just sit for 10 minutes or so, like monks gathered together for silent meditation. Then someone would cautiously break the ice, and more often than not, the conversation that ensued would be utterly different. As if a Quaker meeting were taking place in a corporate setting, self-righteous blustering would be replaced by executives speaking from their hearts as the "spirit" moved them. Often the conversation would drift far afield from the case study as, one after another, the executives "owned up and came clean" about their greatest fears.

Mobley's executive school was an unending series of such experiments, and it is important to note that the goal was not to converge on some preordained "right" answer. Keeping Bill, letting him go, buying him out, transferring him to another department, and any number of other alternatives were still on the table and worthy of consideration. Instead the goal was what the poet T. S. Eliot describes in his *Four Quartets* as "one long purification of motive"—the purification of motive that, Eliot said, leads to "a condition of complete simplicity costing not less than everything," the purification of motive that is essential to achieving authenticity. Rather than arriving at a single "right answer" superimposed by management's superior wisdom, Mobley sought to make sure that all the motivations that usually remain unconscious were brought to the surface so that the hidden biases and agendas that so often distort our decisions could be factored in.

Mobley's approach was built on the notion that self-confidence, willingness to take risks, people orientation, personal accountability, self-criticism, compassion, openness, and all the other values and character traits that great leaders share are merely the by-products—even the unintended consequences—of the authenticity and integrity that comes from self-knowledge.

There was no attempt on Mobley's part to force his students into any predetermined mold. As he put it, "The mission of the IBM Executive School was simply to build an ideal environment for personal growth where participants would become who they really are." And Mobley optimistically believed—as does every religious tradition—that most of what we consider "evil" is merely the by-product of ignorance and fear: ignorance and fear about who we really are.

As for measuring results, Mobley's commitment to the business benefits of self-knowledge and individual authenticity speaks for itself. He was an integral part of the IBM Executive School from

1956 until 1966, and it was his students that turned IBM into the fastest-growing and most admired corporation in the world in the 1960s and 1970s.

Just as it is not necessary or even advisable that we all become monks, you don't need to attend an IBM Executive School to attain self-knowledge. A daily review, religiously practiced, can provide many insights into yourself as you recall your interactions with others and how you behaved in real-life scenarios. Asking friends, colleagues, and family members for a "360 review" will turn them into useful mirrors, revealing those character traits that are too close for you to see. I once offhandedly asked a young SKS student for her opinion of me, and she replied, without hesitation or elaboration, "You are incredibly hard on yourself and other people." This one-sentence summation from a nineteen-year-old girl, compassionately delivered, shocked me to my core—but the realization that she was right forced me to take her words to heart, leaving me forever grateful for her candor.

Rather than seeking comfort in your career or personal life, get acquainted with yourself by seeking new challenges that take you out of your comfort zone. The pressure produced by new challenges doesn't just build character, it also reveals it. It was the pressure of my skydiving accident, for example, that produced the realization that I was far from the person I thought I was, an insight that years of reading and introspection had failed to reveal. While I am, of course, not suggesting anything so drastic as intentionally undergoing a life-threatening accident, pressure, as David Breashears reminds us at the beginning of this chapter, has a remarkable ability to cut through pretense and expose the truth about ourselves. It is one thing to nobly maintain an ethical stance while reviewing a case study in business school. It is quite another to do the same when behaving ethically means losing your house to your creditors.

Finally, find or form a community like the Self Knowledge Symposium or AA that is dedicated to achieving authenticity. As Mobley did for the IBM Executive School, I have developed dozens of experiential exercises for SKS students—such as sitting in the Duke Chapel for five minutes—rather than lecture them. And like Mobley's, the goal is self-discovery rather than merely self-analysis. But most importantly, for the student and adult members of the SKS, putting on an organ recital or even starting a company like RGI were merely our versions of Breashears's high-altitude mountain climbs. These real-life adventures forced us to encounter ourselves and each other in real-life scenarios with something at stake. These encounters produced the "data points" that we later reviewed in the spirit of monastic "recollection" at our weekly meetings.

The best businesspeople don't just sit in endless meetings trying to figure it out. Instead they get out into the marketplace and find out. The same is true for self-knowledge. Reading, introspection, and even think/talk coaching are valuable, but they are no substitute for getting out there and finding out who you really are.

Self-knowledge is essential to making great business decisions. It is the monks' individual authenticity, which arises from addressing the question "Who am I?," that makes them so great at answering the organizational question "Who are we?" And it is the purity of purpose that emerges from this question that gives their monastic business its reputation for authenticity. It is not outright lying or conscious deception that does the most damage to an organization. The real damage arises from self-deception. Well-intentioned people just like you and me are often driven by unconscious fears and hidden agendas—secret agendas so well hidden that they are hidden even from ourselves.

⬭

IN 2000 MY PARTNERS AND I sold Raleigh Group International to an Israeli company called Mutek. Shortly after the acquisition, the board of directors replaced the CEO with a hard-driving executive who seemed downright cold. One day he was visiting our offices in Raleigh and asked to see me.

"I don't get it," he began with a tight smile in accented English, "you invented Visual Intercept and made it the number-one bug-tracking system on the market. I took over six months ago, and it would be fair to say that killing off Visual Intercept is my number-one priority. It's your baby, and your personal contract compensates you on sales of Visual Intercept, yet you haven't raised a single objection—in fact, you've been helping me kill it off. I've been in business thirty years, and I've never seen anything like it. I just have to know why you aren't screaming bloody murder."

"Well, first of all," I said, "I've read your business plan. I agree with it, and I can see why Visual Intercept doesn't fit. Secondly, this company is not about me and my vanity. It's about doing what's best for everybody, and that's what I think your business plan is all about. But most importantly, Visual Intercept isn't me. It's a product, and I have no plans to put the logo on my tombstone."

For a minute or so, the CEO didn't say anything. Then he told me that his father had died when he was three, and that the loving stepfather who had taken his place had died when he was only eleven. These twin losses, he believed, accounted for much of his cold demeanor and his tendency to be emotionally withdrawn. He then spoke of the deep love that he had for his wife and young children, and how determined he was to overcome his fear of abandonment in order to make sure that he would always be there emotionally for his family.

By the time he was finished, I had a completely different take on the man, and our mutual exchange led to a far more productive and open relationship going forward. Three years later my faith in the CEO and his business plan paid off; he flipped our combined companies to a major corporation for $150 million in cash.

As a board member and major stockholder, if I had not gone along with the murder of my "baby," I could have caused a lot of trouble, perhaps enough trouble either to sink the joint venture or at least badly damage its prospects, and if I had, a lot of people—including me—would have suffered tremendously for the sake of my ego. In retrospect this case study contains a number of the monastic lessons we have covered previously.

1. *The truth for the truth's sake.* My Zen teacher, Louis R. Mobley, and the monks of Mepkin shared a love for the truth. Over time they were able to impart this love to me, and this was what made me able to face the fact that Visual Intercept, despite my personal feelings, just didn't fit in.

2. *Detachment.* The monastic virtue of detachment played a major role in this situation. My comment that I had no intention of putting Visual Intercept's logo on my tombstone arose spontaneously and demonstrated that I did not identify with a cardboard box with some software inside. Instead, like the monks and with their help, my life was rooted in something bigger than business, and this allowed me to objectively put a purely business decision into its proper perspective.

3. *Self-knowledge and authenticity.* The CEO's willingness to open up about his life and his motivations allowed us to develop a much more productive and rewarding relationship.

4. *Trust.* Trust in business is everything, and to establish trust, we must have the courage to offer it first, which means exposing our vulnerability. My blanket endorsement of the CEO's business plan, even at the expense of Visual Intercept, demonstrated an enormous amount of loyalty and trust. It also revealed my vulnerability. In effect, I was telling a man I barely knew that he was a lot smarter than I, and trusting him to not take advantage of this admission. The acquisition had been billed as a marriage of equals, and my decision to endorse his business plan meant that this power equation was now altered. Even though I was a board member and had a lot more stock than he did, I had made it clear that I worked for him. Exposing my vulnerability paid off because it, in turn, gave him the feeling of safety he needed to expose his own vulnerability as well.

5. *Every business is a people business.* The details of this case study would never show up in a business-school class. Instead we would learn that the eventual success of our combined companies relied on adroit allocations of capital, serving an underserved market, and creating barriers to competition. All of these factors are important, but in my own experience, success more often relies on the intangibles of interpersonal relationships—relationships that must be built over time and that can't be reduced to a formula. Through more than thirty years of business experience, I have become firmly convinced that a team of people, serving a worthwhile mission and working in an atmosphere of trust, will be successful in just about any business, no matter how competitive or prosaic that business might be. This is exactly what monasteries the world over demonstrate every day.

12

LIVING THE LIFE

ONE DAY I GOT A CALL from Father Stan. Every year the monks of Mepkin undergo a physical, and a routine blood test had revealed that Father Francis, Mepkin's youthful and vibrant abbot, was suffering from an incurable and ultimately fatal form of lymphoma. Chemotherapy could delay the inevitable, but at best Dom Francis had three to five years to live. I felt like the bottom had just dropped out of my life.

A few days later I arrived at Mepkin and made an appointment to meet with Francis. He greeted me affably, and when I asked him how he felt, he grinned and said, "Not bad for a guy who's dying."

I had recently returned from a trip to Israel, where I'd bought a few bottles of wine from a local winery. I offered him one for "medicinal purposes," adding, "It was either this or some holy water from the River Jordan. After praying on it, I opted for the wine."

He laughed and said, "The spirit led you to the right choice."

He told me that the doctors at Memorial Sloan-Kettering in New York had recommended that he hold off on chemo until it was absolutely necessary, since the efficacy of the treatment declined with use. Father Francis had previously agreed to act as a speaker and facilitator at Inward Bound, a three-day conference sponsored by the SKS, for several hundred college students at North Carolina State University, and I told him that if he did not feel up to it, we would more than understand if he decided to cancel.

"No," he said. "I intend to continue with my normal routine for as long as I can. As my health fails, I'll start cutting back, but the last thing to go will be my prayer life."

Several months later Francis arrived at the conference and dove right into working with the students in small group exercises. On the second day, we had lunch together, and while walking back to the conference, he turned to me and said, "Augie, I'm scheduled to give a talk this afternoon. What do you think I should tell the students?"

I gently suggested that since the theme of the conference was authenticity, he should consider telling them about his cancer diagnosis.

"Oh, I don't want to do that," he said, grimacing. "I don't want them to start treating me differently."

"Francis," I countered, "you just told me at lunch how impressed you are by the way the students are baring their souls to you. Are you treating them any differently?"

Francis was quiet for a moment. "Augie," he finally said, "I'm so scared. I'm not scared of dying. I could die tomorrow. It's the chemo. I'm scared to death of the chemo."

A few minutes later, we split up as he headed off to give his talk. I later found out that Father Francis told his story to the students. He didn't hold anything back, and his talk electrified the conference. In survey after survey, students cited his openness and honesty as the most "life-changing" event of the whole conference. My only regrets are that I could not attend and that we failed to record it.

For a couple of years, Francis's immune system held up, but eventually he had to be admitted to Memorial Sloan-Kettering for chemo. Mepkin rented a little apartment across the street from the hospital for him to use between treatments. At first he was slated to be away for a month or so, but as the months dragged on, I contacted Father Stan and asked for permission to visit him in New York. Francis granted my request, but just as I was leaving for New York, I learned that he was back at Mepkin. So I made an appointment to see him through his assistant, Father Kevin, and hurried off to Mepkin instead.

Francis greeted me warmly in his office, and he looked fine. But within minutes his head fell to his chest and he began weeping almost convulsively. When he finally raised his head, he moaned, "Oh, Augie, I was so sick. I was so sick." Spreading his arms he said, "They shoved a thousand needles into each of my arms."

He told me of nausea, sleepless nights, pounding headaches, diarrhea, and ceaseless vomiting for weeks on end. He had grown close to a young man in the bed next to him, only to watch him die from the infections that his shattered immune system could no longer resist. "Almost to the end, he looked fine," he said, "but his immune system was gone."

Again and again Francis was told that he had entered remission. He would be released to his apartment for observation, only to be readmitted a few days later for even harsher chemo when his temperature suddenly spiked. And the ceaseless vomiting would start all over again.

Finally he entered remission yet again and was released to his apartment. It was the holiday season, and he movingly recounted how the Memorial Sloan-Kettering nurses brought him food and Christmas treats in an attempt to alleviate his isolation and loneliness. On Christmas Eve he attended Midnight Mass alone at a local church, and he wept heartsick tears because he missed Mepkin and his brothers so much.

Every day he returned as an outpatient to the hospital to have his temperature taken. If his temperature remained normal for two weeks, he would be allowed to return home. Every day he walked the gauntlet, desperately trying to read his fate in the eyes of a nurse squinting into a thermometer. For eight days his temperature held firm, but then the nurse's face fell. His temperature had spiked yet again, and she had to call the doctor.

"No, no, no," he pleaded, like a man trying to avoid his executioner. "Don't call him yet. Maybe it's an anomaly." Even though it was against procedure, the nurses were so moved by his pleas that they ushered him into a small waiting room. He had two hours: if his temperature returned to normal, he would be released. After two agonizing hours, his temperature was taken again. It was still elevated. The doctor was called, Francis was readmitted, and another round of chemo was prescribed.

But late that night, as he lay awake, unable to sleep, Francis heard a voice saying, "It's time to go home." The next morning he told the doctor and staff that there would be no more treatment. It was time to go home.

As Francis told his story, he relived every agonizing moment of his ordeal, and when he finally repeated, "It was time to go home," he broke down sobbing again.

But suddenly he leaned forward. "Don't talk to me of asceticism," he said fiercely. "You can't choose asceticism. No matter how far out in the desert you go or what sacrifices you make, you always have a choice. You know that if things get too bad, you can always give it up and try something else. But cancer left me no choice but God. What I never could've imagined," he finished softly, "is that my cancer is the answer to a lifetime of prayer."

Several months later Dom Francis Kline died peacefully at home, surrounded by his brothers. At his funeral the governor of South Carolina and other luminaries spoke of his many worldly accomplishments and of the profound effect he'd had on so many people far beyond Mepkin's cloistered walls. But for me, Father Francis's life transcends his worldly accomplishments. These accomplishments are merely the by-products of a man who heroically dared to put God first and let everything else take care of itself. Dom Francis practiced what he preached, trusted the process, and most importantly, faithfully lived the life.

$$\bigcirc$$

THE MOST IMPORTANT SECRET to Mepkin Abbey's business success is the Rule of St. Benedict. At the main monastic midday meal, dinner, the monks eat silently as one of their brothers reads to them from a book chosen by the abbot. At the end of these readings, an excerpt from the Rule is usually added to keep St. Benedict's precepts front and center in the hearts of the community. The most essential and challenging aspect of the Hero's Journey is living the life, and the Rule is a living document used to foster, nurture, and inculcate the values of service and selflessness into the daily life of the monastery.

All aspiring monks go through a long training process called *formation*. They enter as postulants, become novices, take their simple vows, and eventually their solemn vows. Throughout the process their progress is monitored by a novice master and the abbot. A monk's formation is not limited to training sessions, inspirational speeches, and off-site retreats. Formation is a continuous process of peer-to-peer coaching and acculturation designed to make the unnatural values of monastic life so habitual that they become second nature. Despite the watchfulness of the novice master and abbot, the process of formation is primarily bottom up. It is the deeply imbued culture that arises from the Rule of St. Benedict that does most of the heavy lifting of transformation and self-transcendence that spills over into Mepkin's monastic businesses.

As a huge fan of *The Godfather* and *Godfather II*, I shared the general disappointment in the final installment, *Godfather III*. But one scene from the movie is compelling. Michael Corleone goes to a cardinal and is so moved by the goodness of the man that he eventually confesses to ordering the murder of his brother. But what struck me happens before Michael's confession. The cardinal reaches into a fountain nearby, withdraws a rock and breaks it in half. He shows Michael that despite many years surrounded by water, the rock is still completely dry inside. The rock, the cardinal says, is like the hearts of men. Despite centuries surrounded by the waters of Christianity, humanity—and even the Church—are still unaffected. Our hearts are still dry.

Father Christian once told me that if I wanted to "get anywhere spiritually," I had to be "soaked" in St. Thomas Aquinas. But while his taste in philosophers can be hotly debated, if you want to "get anything" from the monks, you must be soaked through and through in the values and principles that guide their lives. Reading this book and a thousand like it will prove of little or no use if you don't commit to living the life. It is only through the long, slow process of living the life that the living waters of spirit permeate our rock-hard heads, until they finally reach our hearts. Once again we will never really learn service and selflessness until we become it.

The first step in living the life is making a commitment. While, as I have said, it is not necessary that we all become monks, making a commitment correlates to a man entering the monastery, determined to become a monk. He has heard his call to the Hero's Journey, overcome his resistance to that call, and made up his mind to turn his back on his "old life" and take the road less traveled toward self-transcendence. Most likely the novice monk has already spent years tweaking his life and trying to smooth out the rough edges, and only now is he ready to admit that a more complete transformation is required. His movement is akin to that of a businessman who, only after vainly spending a lot of time and money trying to tweak his business model, finally faces the fact that he must utterly reinvent the business or eventually face bankruptcy.

Whether it is in business, marriage, getting in shape, getting sober, or taking the Hero's Journey, only an authentic commitment to living the life will bring success. When I was a novice salesman selling 3M copy machines back in 1975, my boss handed me a quotation from W. H. Murray that, he assured me, was the secret to success. I have long since lost that trophy I won for "moving iron," but I've kept that piece of paper all these years because it echoes so neatly what my Zen teacher, Lou Mobley, and later the monks tried to soak into my heart:

> Until one is committed there is hesitancy, the chance to draw back, always ineffectiveness concerning all acts of initiative and creation. There is one elementary truth, the ignorance of which kills countless ideas and splendid plans; that the moment one definitely commits oneself, then providence moves too. All sorts of things occur to help one that would never otherwise have occurred. A whole stream of events issues from the decision raising in one's favor all manner of unforeseen events, meetings and material assistance which no one could've dreamed would have come their way. I have learned a deep respect for one of Goethe's couplets. "Whatever you can do or dream you can, begin it. Boldness has genius, power and magic in it."

This quotation could serve as a summary of the monastic way of life and the secret to the monks' business success. It urges us to overcome our fears, serve something higher, and trust that with boldness, grace—or what Murray calls "providence"—will move as well. Murray and Goethe even allow room for the supernatural as they speak of magical assistance and unforeseen help. When I look back at my own life, everything good that has ever happened to me was a happy accident that resulted from my decision to set out on the Hero's Journey when I was still in college.

I never would have met the monks if it hadn't been for Josh Skudlarick and a broken ankle. And I never would have broken my ankle or met Josh if I hadn't started the SKS, and I never would have learned about the Templeton contest or thought of writing about Brother John if it hadn't been for two SKS students. And I never would have started the SKS and later RGI if I hadn't volunteered to give a lecture about my Zen teacher, and I never would have . . . you get the picture. In one sense my entire life has been completely unplanned, but in another, everything has gone off according to a plan that was just too big for me to see.

I mentioned at the very beginning of this book that my writing career began when I won the John Templeton Foundation's Power of Purpose essay contest. After I won, my youngest brother, Chris, was telling a fellow lawyer about it when his colleague interrupted, "You mean to tell me that your brother never wrote anything in his life . . . then he whips off an essay in a few days and wins 100 grand?"

Chris nodded.

"Wow," he said, "is your brother lucky."

"You don't understand," Chris replied. "My brother has been working on that essay for thirty-five years."

If this sounds like bragging, it couldn't be further from my intention. The single biggest reason why more people don't experience the magic that the monks have to offer is that they believe that while service and selflessness may work for saints, monks, gifted, or "lucky" people, it "won't work for me." It is actually critically important that I convince you that there is nothing essentially "better" about me or the monks you've met in this book. The only difference, such as it is, is having enough faith to act on principles that have surrounded mankind for millennia but that, like the cardinal's rock, never seem to sink in. The most important take-away of this book is that if it can work for me and the monks, it will work for you. All you really need is enough faith to start putting one foot in front of the other.

But if commitment to a higher purpose is the secret to success, there are a few footnotes that I would add to Murray's magnificent manifesto. Intentionally or not, Murray implies that commitment is a static model, a decision that we make once and for all at some unique point in time. But commitment is actually a dynamic model. Commitment may begin with a single decision, but there is all the difference in the world between *making* a commitment and *becoming* committed.

Entering a monastery requires a commitment, but a monk is only committed when he makes his final vows many years later. Making a commitment leads to action, action leads to inspiration, and inspiration leads to an ever-deepening commitment, until one day we wake up to find that we are no longer committing but have become irrevocably committed. Think of it this way: Is a married couple more committed to each other when they say their vows or after they have successfully weathered the ups and downs of a twenty-year marriage? Are we more committed to staying in shape on the day we buy our gym pass or after we have been faithfully attending the gym for years? Commitment, like the Hero's Journey, is a dynamic process, an endless feedback loop that deepens and becomes more perfect over time. Commitment feeds on itself in a virtuous cycle spiraling ever upward.

Unfortunately we humans seem addicted to the idea of a linear, step-by-step approach, without all the messiness that feedback loops bring in their wake. But even the Hero's Journey doesn't work smoothly in a linear, step-by-step fashion. You may very well be returning to help others in business while simultaneously being lost in the Desert of your marriage as you undergo great trials at the hands of your golf swing. The most important lesson here is to be, like a monk, forever mindful. Apply the lens of the Hero's Journey to all aspects of your life, and this will help you sort out what is of ultimate importance from all the background noise and distractions that cloud your judgment. Living the life means staying awake and using the Hero's Journey and service and selflessness as a way of organizing your daily life. The next time you feel overwhelmed at work, ask yourself: Is this all bad, or am I just going through the Desert stage? Is my angst a cue to switch jobs, or merely an essential part of my monklike formation?

But if commitment is central to living the life, there is another aspect that is equally critical. In a previous chapter, I argued that "self-help" and the industry dedicated to its mythology is largely a waste of time. Very few of us have the stamina to "go it alone," especially when we are surrounded by the incessant drumbeat emanating from a society with mostly materialistic goals. On our own, the temptation to march in step with this drumbeat is almost irresistible. As Father Francis said, there is something essentially countercultural about the Hero's Journey, and this is why the monks value community so much that they take a vow of "stability." Similarly, the success of Alcoholics Anonymous relies on providing a countercultural support structure of mutual assistance that goes far beyond AA meetings.

If the example of the monks has resonated with you, then the most important commitment you can make is finding—or creating—a community dedicated to putting monastic principles into practice. In fact, based on my own experience, creating and leading such a community will not only offer you a real-world way to practice service and selflessness but will produce far greater dividends than merely being a member of such a group.

LIVING THE LIFE is just as applicable to business as it is to your personal life. Business success requires having the discipline to faithfully apply the right principles over a long period of time. When I was working for MTV, my boss, John Shaker, started calling me Dr. Follow Up, and I consider that one of the nicest compliments I've ever received. When we started Raleigh Group International, I had always heard that a business was doing well if it kept its bad debt at 3 to 5 percent of total receivables. Partly because I come from a long line of cheapskates, and partly as an exercise in excellence for the sake of excellence, I decided to see if we could do better.

Our terms were "net 30," and I quickly realized that the biggest excuse for late payment was not receiving an invoice. To overcome this objection, we instituted a policy of getting confirmation that our electronic invoice had been received within days of shipping a product. Then our accounts receivable rep would begin calling immediately if we did not receive payment within 30 days. If this proved ineffectual, at 60 days, the receivable was kicked back to the sales rep, and he would pursue collection through the contact who had authorized the purchase. If this didn't work by net 70, our vice president of sales would intervene and move up the chain of command. Finally, if all these measures failed, the receivable would end up on my desk.

Every Monday morning I reviewed our receivables with our accounting department to make sure that each level in our collection process was kicking in on time and being appropriately followed up. But more importantly, my partners and I insisted that we collect our receivables in the spirit of service and selflessness.

When I called a client for collection, I never accused, blustered, or threatened. Instead the first thing I did was ask our client whether he was happy with our product, indicating as I did that we would happily accept the product back if we had failed in any way to deliver on our promises. Only when I had been assured that the customer was happy did I ask why we had never received payment. The only pressure I exerted was the sense that I couldn't understand why, having treated the client fairly, he was in danger of treating us unfairly. Rather than asking for a business decision, I made a personal appeal from one good human being to another to just "do the right thing." We insisted that at every step in our collection process, this philosophy of treating our clients like honorable human beings was adhered to, and the results were almost magical. In seven years in business and without ever running a credit check, we collected all but one of our receivables, and even our lone holdout traded us product in lieu of cash. Not only did we get the money we were owed, but we saved untold thousands on collection agencies and legal fees while avoiding the ill will, negative word of mouth, and permanently lost customers that these harsh remedies invariably bring in their wake.

Our success in collecting our receivables can be attributed to living the life. We were successful because of a rigorous discipline infused with the spirit of service and selflessness. A rigorous discipline meant working our receivables constantly, not in the fits and starts that characterize so many companies that let their receivables "get out of hand." Service and selflessness meant going first and treating others the way we would like to be treated if the tables were turned. Making absolutely certain that the customer was delighted with our product and cheerfully offering to make amends if they were not was the spirit that brought the discipline to life.

Similarly, it is the consistent and methodical tempo of the monastic life that pays off so handsomely for the monks when applied to their businesses. We didn't collect our receivables, we lived our receivables, and, as with the monks, it paid off handsomely for us in the long run as well.

If we want to introduce the magic of service and selflessness in our secular organizations, we must change the daily experience of the workplace. We need corporate missions every bit as powerful as Mepkin's, and the kind of bottom-up culture that lives this mission every day. We must create our own process of formation. We need novice masters who understand that changing the culture is critically important, and we must get the arrows of peer pressure, generated by an authentic community, pointing in the direction of excellence. Above all we need the faith to begin, the commitment to continue, the self-knowledge that reveals how much we need others, and the trust that everything will turn out as it should.

$$\bigcirc$$

DURING ONE OF MY Christmas retreats at Mepkin, Brother Benedict was the designated reader at the monastic midday meal, and the book he was reading aloud to the community at the behest of the abbot was *The Little Prince*. One day he apparently found the book so moving that his reading was continually interrupted by his own sobbing. Each time, however, he managed to pull himself together and continue reading. After the short monastic service of None that follows dinner and takes place in the refectory, I approached Brother Benedict as he was eating his deferred and well-earned lunch.

"Jesus, Augie," he said, "I don't know what came over me. If it hadn't been for Michael Jackson, I never would've made it. Every time I started going to pieces, I just kept repeating 'Michael Jackson, Michael Jackson.' Imagining Michael in his Moon Boots took my mind off the book just long enough to be able to get through it."

As a monastic guest, I have the privilege of living and working with the monks and sharing their life. The only exception is that monastic guests are, understandably, excluded from meetings, or "chapters," at which the community discusses more private matters. One of these private chapters takes place on New Year's Day, and a few days after Brother Benedict's reading, Father Francis, quite unexpectedly, invited me to attend. The meeting was held in the reading room, liberally stocked with newspapers and magazines, adjoining the infirmary. Chairs were drawn up in a circle, and when I entered, Francis motioned for me to sit at his right hand.

A huge box of Godiva chocolates, a Christmas present from a grateful retreatant, magically appeared and was passed around the room. Then Francis, starting at his left, asked each monk to comment on the events of the past year and their hopes for the next. When everyone had had their say, there was no one left but me. Father Francis turned to me with a big smile and said, "So, what do you have to say for yourself, Brother Augie?"

I was so obviously moved by this unexpected gesture of acceptance that the entire community erupted in laughter. I was so tongue-tied that the only thing I remember is glancing over at Brother Benedict and hissing, "Michael Jackson, Michael Jackson." I am extremely grateful for all the blessings I have received in my life, but none means more to me than being called Brother Augie that one time by Dom Francis, in the midst of all my heroes. It felt like after a long and harrowing journey I had finally made it home safe and sound.